Contents

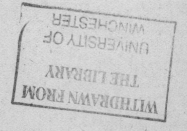

Editors' Preface

Recent decades have witnessed unprecedented advances in research on human development. Each book in *The Developing Child* reflects the importance of this research as a resource for enhancing children's well-being. It is the purpose of the series to make this resource available to that increasingly large number of people who are responsible for raising a new generation. We hope that these books will provide rich and useful information for parents, educators, child-care professionals, students of developmental psychology and all others concerned with childhood.

JEROME BRUNER, *University of Oxford*
MICHAEL COLE, *University of California, San Diego*
BARBARA LLOYD, *University of Sussex*

1/Three Questions

One of us teaches a course entitled 'Child Language', and it was one of the courses in the college catalogue, among other esoteric offerings such as 'Lichens of the Arctic' and 'The Polish Verb', that was gently ridiculed in a student publication: next to the course title the author had drawn a cartoon depicting a mindless-looking baby saying 'ba-ba' into a microphone held by several serious, scholarly adults. The cartoon came unnervingly close to the truth, for collecting transcripts of child speech is an enterprise that makes one feel rather foolish at times. But it continues to supply deep insights into language learning, and this phenomenon, which normally occurs among all infants in the world (and proceeds equally well whether scholarly adults listen closely or not), continues to be one of the most exciting things that a young child does. Parents are delighted by their infant's progress from helplessness to independence, but other markers of progress, such as crawling, walking, or drinking from a cup, pale in comparison to the first true words. Like most things children do, language attracts the greatest attention when it is wrong. A child calls everyone on two legs 'Daddy' or says 'ephelant' or 'his is gooder than mine'. These conspicuous errors of speech provide a glimpse into the remarkable task of language learning that is the business of early childhood.

The emergence of language is exciting because it is a reflection of what the child knows. Moreover, once language is present, it increases, or at least refines, that knowledge. Language provides a window on the child's mental abilities: by studying how he* speaks we get some idea of what he knows. But in spite of all the research over the past fifteen years, the acquisition of language remains something of a mystery: how, precisely, does it happen?

In an attempt to solve the puzzle, three questions recur. First, *how does the child learn language so well in so short a time?* It makes sense to begin with the experiences a child actually has. In Western society, language is normally learned from adults – but could a child learn it from his young brother or sister? What if a child is deaf, or retarded, or if his parents are deaf – how does that affect his ability to learn the language? What if he is raised in a bilingual household, exposed to two languages at the same time? Are 'teachers' necessary at all – or can children learn as well by listening to a radio or watching television?

Clearly, some proportion of language learning involves imitation: the American child learns to greet a friend by saying 'Hello', the Zulu child by saying 'Tsa bona'. But there is more involved here than learning the sounds that symbolize a greeting, or any of the other concepts in human thought. Language is a game played by precise rules. A phrase like 'his is gooder than mine' tells us a lot about the machinery at work that processes what is heard: since it is not used in adult speech, the child does not hear it and therefore cannot be imitating it. Although wrong, the phrase uses a familiar rule ('his is faster than mine'). The phrases suggest that the child – quite unconsciously – is extracting regularities (or rules) from what he hears and applying them to compose his own utterances. Experiences

---

* We have used the male pronoun generically because it seemed awkward to do otherwise.

from the outside and a capacity within the child, then, must both mesh for language to occur. We will trace what is currently known – and what remains to be learned – about these processes.

Innate capacity as a prerequisite for language raises another issue: must one be human to learn language? Human beings walk upright, laugh, and have a grip made superior by possession of a thumb. Historically, though, no behaviour has been considered so defining of the species as language, and since Descartes the answer to this question had been an unequivocal yes. In recent years the answer has become less certain. As it turns out, chimpanzees not only have thumbs but several have demonstrated that they can, indeed, learn to use symbols and play by linguistic rules with a sophistication that rivals that of a two-year-old child, and no one yet knows where the chimpanzees will stop. Whether language is a uniquely human venture depends upon one's definition of language, and that definition has become increasingly refined. In our final chapter, we debate this question and others having to do with the specific characteristics of human language learning.

What is the course of language learning? Parents, like linguists, are curious about what a child knows at different times, how that knowledge changes, and what typical errors are made. Recent work has shown that much important learning about language goes on before the child ever starts to talk, and our study begins here. The infant learns to pay attention to speech, he listens for critical sound changes, he attends to the rhythm and intonation of talking long before he knows what it means. For instance, children prepare for the alternation involved in conversation – first I talk then you talk – by playing games such as peek-a-boo, where two people are held together in a common activity but play different parts: one is active, the other observes, and then the roles are reversed.

Although the child's first word may not appear until the age of one, or later, he is engaged throughout his first year in elaborate nonverbal rituals with his caregiver that lay the groundwork for true conversations. Our story will end at school age because by the age of six the child's language is in many respects like an adult's.

Month by month a child masters new vocabulary and discovers, then applies, new grammatical rules. But fascinating though they are, vocabulary and grammar are not all that the child learns. His central concern is communication and interaction with other people, and language mirrors his sensitivity to the perspective and knowledge of his listeners. During the preschool period language gains flexibility until, in any given situation, the child has many options of style, manner, and grammatical form that he can use for his own purposes. Along with greater flexibility comes greater reflection: there is a steady improvement in ability to think about language, to treat it as an entity, and to gain conscious control over the medium itself. A two-year-old uses words without knowing *what* a word is. A five-year-old can talk about words and the games he can play with them. Formal schooling brings the first demands on this new consciousness of language, as the child learns to read and write. We shall describe the origins of these significant changes in the preschool years and speculate about the early foundations of literacy.

How do you figure out what a child knows? You might think that all you need to do is look and listen, and in fact that is how the study of language acquisition began. Since the nineteenth century, linguists have taken a professional as well as parental interest in what their children were saying and have kept diaries of their spontaneous speech. Some of the most extensive samples of child speech were recorded in this century by linguists studying their own children: a thorough study of French by Antoine Grégoire, a lengthy work on German by Werner Leopold, and diaries of English learning by several writers such as A. F. and J. C. Chamberlain and H. V. Velten.[1] This method has its advantages: it is longitudinal in nature, so that the process of one child's learning becomes evident; moreover, the study is conducted by a person who best knows the child, with all his past history, routines, and idiosyncrasies. It also has some disadvantages – the record is often patchy so that one cannot be sure how representative the diary is of that child's speech in general, and whether the findings are true for other children.

More recently, researchers began to collect samples of children's speech with a tape recorder. They hoped that by recording a sizeable amount of speech at one time, they could get a large enough sample of utterances to figure out how the child's knowledge of his language changed over time. Although a number of sampling strategies have been tried, one very popular method is to record everything the child says for an hour or two once a week. Typically, samples from several children are compared and subjected to intensive analysis: everything the children say is written down and tabulated and tallies are made of the words, the grammatical rules, the varieties of sentences, and so forth.

Besides expanding sampling techniques, other linguists have taken a slightly different approach. In the early 1960s it was recognized that children might not learn merely an incomplete version of adult grammar, but might instead invent rules of their own. So linguists began trying to 'crack the code' of children's speech exactly as if they were encountering, for the first time, a language spoken by some remote Indian tribe. It became evident that they faced an obstacle that other anthropological linguists do not. In studying a strange language, investigators usually have an informant who speaks the language, can answer their questions, and determine when their interpretations are correct. Children, however, make very poor informants, so their speech has to stand as the only source of information.

Furthermore, just when one decides upon a grammar, the child will go and change the rules, for the language of the child is not static but changing.

But the most serious problem with this method is that it can misrepresent what the child really knows. Since he is concerned with communicating *meanings* to the people around him, the written transcript must include notes on what the child is *doing* while he talks and on what is being said to him. His proficiency at encoding these meanings into the conventional words and sentences of his language can only be assessed if one knows (from the context) what he is trying to express and whether (from the reaction of his listeners) he succeeds. The focus on 'language in context', therefore, has engendered a whole new technology of videotapes, frame-by-frame film analysis, and elaborate scoring manuals for gestures and eye movement.

Study of spontaneous speech, though central to research on language acquisition, is not the only method available to the psychologist. Often an idea arises that can then be tested in an experiment. Perhaps the best kind of experiment, with the fewest loopholes, tests the child's comprehension. Comprehension tests fall into two major categories: those that ask the child to choose among pictures or objects and those that require him to act out something. But the test designer must be alert to ensure that he is discovering what the child really knows. Suppose one wanted to find out if a child understood the word *horse*. It would not be enough to ask him to choose among pictures of a horse, teacup, tree, and banana, since he might guess correctly but still not understand that the word *horse* is restricted to horses. He might think it meant *animal*, for instance, and be just as likely to pick out a dog or a cow if they were offered as alternatives. Moreover, young children have great difficulty scanning a number of pictures and often do not follow the instruction 'look carefully at *each one* and tell me which one I'm talking about'. Instead they tend to stare at one – or always pick the one in the left-hand corner. Very young children can deal with no more than two pictures, and even three-year-olds have trouble with four pictures. Unfortunately, the fewer pictures offered, the less certain one can be that the child truly understands, for he may be guessing or he may fail if offered other alternatives.

Acting out may require other skills. For example, a child has to 'make the horse kick the cow' using toy animals. If he has had little opportunity to engage in pretend play with toy animals, he may be at a serious disadvantage. But if he does act it out correctly, there is less uncertainty about the child's knowledge than there is with a picture test. What must be guarded against, in this case, is asking the child to do something he was probably going to do anyway. If you hand a small child a cup and a ball and tell him 'Put the ball *in* the cup', he is almost sure to obey. If you tell him 'Put the cup *over* the ball', on the other hand, he is almost sure to fail. This does not necessarily mean that he understands *in* but not *over*; it is just that if you leave him alone you will see that his dominant response when confronted with a container is to put an object in it. So the natural repertoire of the child must be taken into account in designing tests of comprehension.

Comprehension-test results frequently come as a surprise to parents. As a rule, they see their child acting in ordinary situations where no one has troubled to avoid helpful cues, to make sure the alternatives are confusing, or to take into account what the child is likely to do anyway. The natural circumstances of language learning inevitably support understanding. Only when they are stripped away can the clear limits of the child's language understanding be defined.

Another kind of test capitalizes on the child's tendency to imitate. The method can tell us something about speech

sounds. For instance, a young child may never spontaneously produce an /f/ sound in his own speech – but it may
be that he never had occasion to do so. If he can be
induced to attempt to imitate the words *frog, fish* and *fire*,
his imitations will answer the question of whether he has
an /f/ in his repertoire. The method can also reveal the
kinds of sentences the child is capable of forming or what
he hears of complex adult sentences. Consider the following imitations of one two-year-old girl.[2]

Adult: The owl eats candy and runs fast.
Child: Owl eat candy . . . owl eat the candy and . . .
      he run fast.
Adult: The man who I saw yesterday runs fast.
Child: I saw the man who run fast.
Adult: The boy the chair hit was dirty.
Child: Boy hit the chair was dirty.

Nevertheless, imitated sentences are not always exactly like
those a child might produce by himself, since asking a child
to imitate a long sentence out of its normal context places
a strain on his memory. The following dialogue is an
example of one child's attempts to imitate sentences spoken
by an adult.[3]

Adult: I'm trying to get this cow in there.
Child: Cow in here.
Adult: I'm gonna get the cow to drink milk.
Child: Get the cow to drink milk.
Adult: You made him stand up over there.
Child: Stand up there.

Although the child could not succeed, all of the sentences
spoken by the adult were sentences the child himself had
produced the previous day. The difference was that the

child's spontaneous speech had been in appropriate contexts of play.

A third kind of experiment stimulates the child to say something himself. Jean Berko invented a production test that has become known as 'the wug test' because it introduced new words like *wug* to name various novel things, actions, and qualities shown in cartoon form.⁴ The purpose of the test is to see whether children have mastered the English rules for making plurals, past tenses, and so on, and can generalize them to new words. In one case, the child is shown a funny bird-type creature and is told, 'This is a wug. Now there's another one. There are two . . . ?' If the child correctly answers 'wugs', one can be sure he knows how to make plurals because he could never have heard that word from anyone else. In another cartoon, a man is playing with a kind of yo-yo, and the researcher says, 'This is a man who knows how to bod. He did the same thing yesterday. Yesterday he . . . ?' When a child answers 'bodded', he must know how to create the past-tense form of a new verb.

Another production test is played out with puppets, one held by the researcher and the other by another adult. They model a game in which one puppet, say, argues with everything the other puppet says. If one puppet says 'He likes bananas', the second says 'He doesn't like bananas', and children are usually delighted by the escalating verbal warfare. After a few examples the child is asked if he would like to work the argumentative puppet. Very few refuse. Using this game one can tell whether the child knows how to make the negative form of a wide variety of sentences, selected by the researcher.

These descriptions are intended to be a quick review of the methods used by linguists and psychologists to find out what children know. Parents, curious to see how they might apply to their own children, may want to try out one or two experiments with simple materials and toys. But the main purpose of this survey is to give some idea of the variety and scope of efforts to explore the language of the developing child. The efforts are becoming more discerning, but we are only beginning to understand the complexity of early language learning. In the first two years alone, the child makes a leap that recapitulates evolutionary developments several aeons in the making – but it is a leap, as we shall begin to see in the next chapter, that is actually composed of many little steps.

2/Sounds

In the first two years the child is transformed from a helpless, self-absorbed infant, whose waking life seems dominated by the acquisition and elimination of food and drink, into a mobile, inquisitive, and communicative toddler who has developed a mind of his own and is now preoccupied with exploring his social and physical environment. The two most striking changes in this period are the onset of walking and the emergence of speech, events that are typically quite closely meshed in time. The child usually takes his first hesitant steps and utters his first understandable words towards the end of the first year or early in the second. A major factor in advances in locomotion and vocalization seems to be the physical maturity of the child. Malnutrition and various types of mental retardation that slow the maturation of the child's brain tend to slow down his progress through the motor milestones of sitting, crawling, standing, and walking, and the development of vocal communication to about the same degree. Nevertheless, it is not too remarkable to find a chatty one-year-old who still spends more time on his bottom than on his feet, or a budding sprinter at fifteen months who has little to say for himself.

In this chapter and the next we shall examine the emergence of the first words, considering how physical maturation and the child's environment affect the rate and pattern of word learning. Three major questions about children's first words will concern us:

1. What do the first words sound like and how do they relate to the child's preverbal vocalizations?
2. What do the first terms of reference mean, for the child and for the adult, and how does the adult's speech to the child influence which words are learned first?
3. What functions do the early words serve in communication, and how do they relate to the nonverbal interaction between parent and child?

HEARING SPEECH SOUNDS

We begin with the sounds of speech, for it is here that the child must also begin. From the first he is exposed to a wide variety of noises from his environment, including the complex sounds directed at him by other people. To decipher the messages that those sounds contain the child must separate the noises he hears into speech and non-speech, and then divide up the speech into words and the individual sounds that form them. Most of the coos, grunts, clicks and wheezes that may accompany speech, and some of the variation in the speech sounds themselves, can be ignored, for they do not affect the messages being communicated; but other subtle differences in sound alter the meaning of words and sentences. For example, many words in English are distinguished by just one consonant or vowel sound. Consider the set *bin, din, fin, gin, kin, pin, sin, shin, tin, thin* and *win*; these words differ only in their initial consonants. The set *pan, pen, pin, pun* and *pawn* differs only in their vowels. The speech sounds of a language that contrast with one another in this way indicate changes in meaning and are called *phonemes*.

Linguists place them inside oblique strokes (/b/, /d/, /g/) to distinguish them from the letters of the alphabet and from speech-sound changes that do not affect the meaning of words. In order to be understood the child must learn to hear and pronounce the phonemes of his language with reasonable accuracy.

To complicate the task for the child, the sound changes that distinguish between phonemes, and hence between words, vary from language to language. Pronunciation of the /t/ sound in English varies in breathiness (aspiration) depending on the word in which it appears. In *stop* there is comparatively little air expelled with the /t/, but in *top* there is more – the reader can verify this by saying the two words up against the back of the hand. Yet differences in aspiration do not contrast words in English; *stop* pronounced with the breathy /t/ of *top* still has the same meaning. In contrast, the degree of aspiration of /t/, /p/ and /k/ is crucial for distinguishing between words in languages like Zulu, Hindi, and Arabic. The Zulu word tusa means 'to praise', but *thusa* with a breathy /t/ means 'to frighten'.

On the other hand, English makes some distinctions between phonemes that are not made in other languages. Words such as *zip* and *sip* contrast in meaning, so /z/ and /s/ are separate phonemes in English. But in Spanish there is no contrast in meaning carried by /z/ and /s/ so they are not different phonemes. Similarly, Japanese native speakers do not distinguish between sounds in the range of our /r/ and /l/, although they do produce speech sounds that approximate to those consonants. The child learning a particular language comes to hear and produce with accuracy the sound differences that change meaning and ignores those variations that are not functional in his language. Adult English speakers come to ignore aspiration so well that they have difficulty in learning to hear and produce the different /t/, /k/ and /p/ phonemes in Zulu.

Similarly, a failure to distinguish /r/ and /l/ is part of our stereotype of Japanese speakers learning English.

Children do not, however, come completely unprepared to the task of discriminating between speech sounds. Within a matter of days after birth, they are highly responsive to speech or other sounds of similar pitch to the human voice. In fact, speech seems to be rewarding to the infant in a way that other sounds are not. Newborns will learn to suck on an artificial nipple hooked to a switch that turns on a brief portion of recorded speech or vocal music, but they will not suck as readily in order to hear instrumental music or other rhythmical sounds.[1] In the first few months of life, speech elicits greater electrical activity in the left half of the child's brain and music elicits greater activity in the right half of the brain, as is the case with adults.[2] This suggests that at a very early age the two hemispheres of the brain are already specialized for dealing with the different kinds of sound. So from the beginning of infancy children are able to discriminate speech from nonspeech, and they seem to pay particular attention to speech.

Still more important, young infants are especially sensitive to some sound differences that distinguish between words in many languages. For example, one way that English speakers produce different phonemes is by varying the time between moving the lips and vibrating the vocal cords. In speaking a /b/, for instance, the vocal cords vibrate just as the lips open, but in the case of /p/ the lips move fractions of a second before the vocal cords are set in motion. The time at which the vocal cords vibrate is known as the voice onset-time, or VOT: /b/ has a VOT of 0 milliseconds, because there is no delay, /p/ has a VOT of +40 milliseconds. In all other respects the two sounds are highly similar. The same time difference distinguishes /d/ from /t/ and /g/ from /k/.

Does it require lengthy exposure to a language to hear this minute difference between consonants, or are we innately equipped to hear it? Studies with preverbal infants disclose that they can discriminate sounds like /b/ and /p/ at a very early age.[3] The most effective demonstration takes advantage of the finding that infants will suck on a nipple to hear speech. Provided that the baby sucks with sufficient force he is played a tape of the syllable /ba/ following each suck. After a few minutes of this he appears to tire of the sound and the rate of sucking declines rapidly. At this point the syllable is changed to /pa/. If the child cannot tell the difference between the two sounds the rate of sucking should continue to decline, as it does if one continues to play the /ba/ syllable. But with infants as young as a few weeks old the rate of sucking jumps to high levels immediately following the change, indicating that the child can distinguish between the old /ba/ and the new /pa/.

Infants and English-speaking adults can readily detect small differences in VOT in the region of +25 to +40 milliseconds, but they are insensitive to larger differences in VOT at other points along the time continuum. For example, if one sound has a VOT of +40 milliseconds and another has a VOT of +100 milliseconds, we hear them both as /p/, and so do infants. This suggests that the human ear has a region of special sensitivity in the region of +25 to +40 milliseconds of VOT, and many languages have taken advantage of that sensitivity by placing the boundaries between several consonants at that point. The child embarks upon the task of language learning innately prepared to distinguish small variations in sound that will change the meanings of many words.

Nevertheless, a few languages place phoneme boundaries outside this region of special sensitivity. Thai, for instance, has a /b/ like that of English; but it also has a pre-voiced /mb/, for which the vocal cords are vibrated some 50 milliseconds before the mouth is opened (that is, the boundary between /b/ and /mb/ is around a VOT of *minus* 50 milliseconds). Infants cannot distinguish the pre-voiced /mb/ from a /b/ until they have had considerable exposure to the Thai language.

The delicate timing of the ear in making these distinctions is worth noting. Delays no longer than 40 milliseconds in the onset of voicing distinguish /b/ from /p/, /d/ from /t/ and /g/ from /k/. Similarly, rapid changes in sound frequency that last for only 25 to 50 milliseconds separate /b/ from /d/ and /d/ from /g/. Unfortunately some children experience great difficulty in hearing brief changes in sound or detecting small differences in time intervals, although by other measures they do not appear to be deaf.[4] These children are called dysphasic. They are severely hampered in their acquisition of English because they cannot distinguish between many consonant sounds like the above.

Although the normal infant is very sensitive to voice onset-time differences between /b/ and /p/, /d/ and /t/, and so on, he must still learn that these differences are important for distinguishing between words in his native language. Only towards the end of the second year, when the child understands several words and even has a few in his own productive vocabulary, can he use differences in voicing to contrast words that label objects. We can demonstrate this by presenting the child with two funny toys made up to look like people. Each object is given a nonsense syllable name, such as *bok* and *pok*, chosen so that they differ only by the initial consonant. The child is then invited to do things with each object, such as 'Let pok take a ride on the wagon' or 'Put the hat on bok'. Although one-month-old infants can detect the sound difference between /b/ and /p/, children under eighteen months have little success in picking out the correct object in the *bok-pok* task.[5] It is not that they cannot associate a nonsense syllable label with an object or cannot carry out the actions, because they have no problem when the difference between labels is made more distinct, for example, *bok* and *zav*. They simply have not yet learned that a difference in VOT like that between /b/ and /p/ signals a difference in reference.

To summarize, infants are responsive to speech at a remarkably early age and can make fine discriminations between a number of speech sounds. However, the child must learn which of the many discriminable differences in speech sounds actually function to mark differences in reference in his native language. This requires considerable exposure to the language and is not complete even at the end of the second year.

PRODUCING SPEECH SOUNDS

At three or four months of age babies begin cooing and babbling sounds that approximate speech. The babbling increases in frequency until it peaks between nine and twelve months. Although it often occurs in sentencelike sequences with rising and falling intonations, babbling remains uninterpretable to parents. At about a year children produce their first understandable words, often reduplicated syllables like *mama*, *dada*, or *papa*, or single consonant-vowel syllables like *da* for *dog* or *ba* for *baby*. For some children babbling ceases when the first words appear, but other children continue to produce long babbled sentences even while their intelligible vocabulary grows. We observed a delightful instance of this while making a movie on language acquisition for the Canadian Broadcasting Corporation. We were filming an eighteen-month-old girl, Katie, to illustrate the one-word stage of speech. Katie obligingly produced with great clarity and apparent effort the single words *book* and *look* while leafing through a large picture book with her mother. But then she picked up her own little book and began to 'read' it, uttering long sentences of nonsense complete with elaborate intonation. To our amusement the cameraman then zoomed in on Katie, to reveal to the viewers that all the time her book had been upside down. Katie clearly knew that there was more involved in reading than uttering single words, no matter how precisely they were pronounced.

But children's use of babbled sentences is not confined to imitations of reading. Some children seem determined not to let their desire to communicate be frustrated by their lack of words. It can be most disconcerting to have a fifteen-month-old who you know can manage only a handful of English words come through from an adjoining room, look you in the eye, point back into the other room, and say: 'Gonggong dingdong baba da?' You cannot escape the feeling that the child has created a language of his own and if you possessed an English-Childish dictionary he would tell you something quite profound.

Surprisingly, there has been almost no study of the babbled sentences of children who can already say a few words even though such study might illuminate the child's early mastery of speech. For example, is any aspect of the babbling consistent across similar circumstances? Do the same word-like sequences turn up in the same eliciting circumstances? This kind of consistency would suggest that the child constructs his own words for objects and events at the same time that he learns words from the adults around him. A few children do seem to do this; it is not uncommon to hear parents say something like 'That's Sam's word for spaghetti' after the child has uttered something that sounds to the naïve listener more like a burp than a word.

Even if the speech sounds vary from occasion to occasion, does the intonation pattern of the babbled sentences seem to be appropriate to their apparent communicative intent? Are questions distinguishable from statements, for example? Infants as young as six to eight months old notice the difference between a rising and falling intonation pattern over a syllable or phrase,[6] but there is no evidence that those patterns function to distinguish a query from a statement until much later. In the one-word stage children do come to use intonation to signal different intentions – demands, questions, statements and so on – but the intonation patterns he uses do not always correspond to those used by adults in their simple sentences to the child. One wonders if some children use intonation in their babbled sentences before they apply them to their single-word utterances.

These questions are part of a larger issue: what is the relationship between babbling and the child's first words? The child babbles a wide variety of speech sounds, some of which do not occur in the language he is learning, although they may be found in other languages. Thus a child who hears only English may nevertheless produce a click sound that is used extensively in Southern African languages but never appears in English. Or he may make a sound by blowing through his lips like a cross between a /p/ and an /f/; this appears in Japanese but is decidedly not English. On the other hand, the child may not babble many sounds that are quite frequent in his native language. Some sounds therefore drop out while others appear for the first time in the transition from babbling to words.

One theory of speech development suggests that the child's language comes to approach that of adult speakers by two processes. First, parents selectively reward those sounds that approximate the speech sounds of their language by paying attention, smiling, or responding verbally to them and not to other sounds. Second, the child imitates the speech he hears from others. A more sophisticated version of this theory argues that the child associates his mother's voice with the good feelings of comfort, warmth and food. Thereafter his own speech is rewarding to him to the extent that it sounds like his mother's.[7] Hence imitation is itself rewarding. There are elements of truth in this theory. Children clearly learn to pronounce words correctly by comparing their own productions with those of the adults around them. Furthermore, young children are accomplished mimics of the behaviour and speech of their parents and do attempt to imitate the words they hear. Even the pitch of a child's voice shifts to match that of the person to whom he is talking; it is higher when he interacts with a woman and lower when he interacts with a man.[8] Finally, social and vocal reward does increase the frequency of babbling.[9] Even deaf children babble for longer if they can see an adult responding to their vocalizations, although they cannot hear their own sounds or the adult's vocal response.

Nevertheless, such a theory is at best incomplete, for it leaves out important determinants of speech development in children. There are constraints on the rate and pattern of sound development in babbling and in the early words which depend more on the maturing control of the child over his articulatory organs than on the frequency of the speech sounds in parental speech or on any rewards the child receives for producing those sounds. The onset of babbling seems to be a matter of physical maturation rather than exposure to speech, since deaf children begin to babble at about the same age as hearing children. However, continuation of babbling past eight or nine months of age depends on being able to hear oneself and others. Profoundly deaf children usually stop babbling at about that age and seldom learn to produce words.

The developmental pattern of babbling is also very similar across different languages, so that French, Japanese and English babies all sound alike at this stage.[10] The child begins by producing guttural consonant sounds like /g/ and /k/ at the back of the mouth, and vowels like /a/ near the middle of the mouth. The range of babbled vowels then expands to include those pronounced near the front or back of the mouth, but the guttural consonants tend to disappear and be replaced by sounds like /b/, /p/ and /d/ which are produced at the teeth and lips. This change in the dominant consonant sounds cannot be explained by selective reward or imitation because there would be no reason for the perfectly appropriate /g/ and /k/ sounds to drop out of the child's repertoire if, for example, he were learning English. Social and vocal rewards increase the amount of babbling, but they have little, if any, effect on the range of sounds babbled. Even when nine-month-old children are exposed to a concentrated input of syllables containing a wider variety of consonants than they themselves produce, they do not immediately broaden the range of consonants that they babble, although they babble more frequently.[11] It is only at the very end of the period of babbling that language input begins to influence the child's speech, and here the different languages begin to be distinguished.

Emergence of the first words at ten to fifteen months is determined as much by the child's control of articulation as by his ability to associate labels with objects. Most children can understand and respond appropriately to a number of words before they can produce any. Furthermore, the few deaf children who have been studied learning sign language from their parents produced their first signed words for objects around eight months, somewhat earlier than speaking children, presumably because at that age gestural signs are easier to make than words are to articulate. But the consistency of the speech input can also be an important influence on the age at which a child utters his first words and the speed at which he learns words. Children exposed to two or more languages from the beginning tend to be a little slower in their early vocabulary development because each object and event is paired with more than one word. However, they soon catch up with children learning a single language.

The change from babbling to words represents a shift from unconstrained practice or play with sounds (where there is no necessity for the child to produce any particular sound following any other) to planned, controlled speech. The child must produce particular speech sounds in sequence to make the words intelligible to his hearer. In fact children greatly simplify the pronunciation of their early words. For a while many children regularize all multi-syllable words to reduplicated syllables – for example, a child might say *bubba* for *button*, *butter*, *bubble* and *baby*, making use of context vital for understanding what he is referring to. At the same time, all single-syllable words may be reduced to a consonant plus a vowel: *du* for *duck*, *be* for *bed*, and so on. To some extent adults' baby talk to children provides simplified models that fit this mould, words like *mama*, *dada*, *weewee*, *booboo* and *choochoo*.

Nevertheless, amid the fragmented early words there may be the isolated words that the child pronounces flawlessly. At fifteen months our son Nicholas produced a perfect *turtle* for the various toy turtles that swam with him in his bathtub. Later on, when the child begins to form systematic strategies or rules for the pronunciation of words, these 'progressive idioms' are brought into line with the new patterns of pronunciation. So at eighteen months Nicholas's *turtle* became *kurka*. Another example is provided by Hildegard, the daughter of the linguist Werner Leopold.[12] Between ten and sixteen months Hildegard pronounced the word *pretty* in a remarkably adult manner; but at eighteen months *pretty* became *biddy*, in keeping with the way she said other words at that time.

Sometimes the child understands several words beginning with or containing a particular type of speech sound, but for a period of time he makes no attempt to produce them. Since there is nothing that the words have in common besides the sounds they share, the child appears to be actively avoiding words containing certain speech sounds and selectively producing those sounds he has mastered.

Some of the pronunciation errors that children make in their first words may arise from mishearing the adult words, especially in the case of multisyllable words. The accurate perception of speech sounds develops over the second and third years, and misperceptions of similar sounding words occasionally occur, especially if the child knows the meaning of only one of the words. Nicholas at fourteen months had learned what *comb* meant and, whenever he came across one, would attempt to comb the precious few strands of hair he possessed at the time. One day he found a pine cone outside and brought it to his mother. 'What a lovely cone,' she said to him, whereupon he tried to comb his hair with it. At about the same age he confused the words *rape* and *grape*, but we will leave the details of that incident to the reader's imagination. Generally, however, the child's perception of words seems to be much better than his production of them. A child might use the word *maus* for both *mouth* and *mouse*, or *guck* for both *truck* and *duck*, yet quite easily pick out the appropriate referents for those words.

When the child has acquired about fifty words he begins to adopt quite regular patterns of pronunciation, some of which are found in children learning any language. This leads to consistent errors in pronunciation, some arising from the systematic deletion of parts of the adult word, others taking the form of the substitution of certain sounds for the correct adult sounds. For example, it is fairly universal that children in the early stages of language development reduce the consonant clusters that begin words, usually to a single consonant. So *spoon* becomes *poon*, *smack* is reduced to *mack*, and so on. Consonant clusters are one of the last aspects of the sound system of English to be mastered, and some children continue to ience difficulty with them until four or five years of

other common strategy that children employ to simplify the pronunciation of words is the assimilation of all the consonants or vowels in a word to the same place of articulation in the mouth. This process can operate in either direction, with the initial consonant being changed to correspond to the place of articulation of the final consonant, as in *goggy* for *doggy*, or the opposite, *doddy* for doggy.

Finally, young children have a preference for initial consonants that are accompanied by vibration of the vocal cords (voicing) and for final consonants that are not voiced. They therefore tend to replace unvoiced consonants like /p/, /t/ and /k/ with their voiced counterparts /b/, /d/ and /g/ at the beginning of words, but do just the opposite at the ends of words. So a child will say *bie* for *pie*, *doe* for *toe* and *bop* for *pop*; but at the same time pronounce *knob* as *knop* and *dog* as *dok*. Frequently several of the simplifying principles will operate at once in the child's pronunciation of a word. The use of *guck* for *truck* and *beep* for *creep* represents the combination of all three of the above principles. The initial consonant cluster is reduced from two consonants to one, the first and last consonants are produced at the same point in the mouth (/g/ and /k/ at the back of the mouth, /b/ and /p/ at the lips) and the first consonant is voiced.

In short, the errors of omission and substitution that two-year-olds make in their attempts to produce adult words are not random, but follow systematic patterns. Many other simplifying principles have been observed,[13] and individual children may differ as to which of the principles they adopt or which of them predominate at different stages of language development. But the principles we have looked at here are widespread across children and across languages, and all children may demonstrate one or more of them.

A close relationship exists between babbling and the pronunciation of the early words. Many of the simplifying principles used by children reflect the preferences for certain sounds or sound combinations that develop in the latter part of the period of babbling.[14] In babbling, there are very few consonant clusters, reduplicated syllables are common, and initial consonants outnumber final ones two to one. Further, initial consonants tend to be voiced but final consonants are unvoiced. All of these are common patterns in the early words as well. The maturing control of the child over his speech organs may therefore not only determine the sound preferences that emerge in later babbling but also constrain the types of errors and substitutions the child makes in his first words.

One final observation is worth making about the sound of the early words. It is tempting to assume that the child's pronunciation of words differs from that of adults because he is unable to produce certain sounds or particular sound combinations. To some extent this is true, but it is not always correct. The speech of Amahl, the son of the English linguist Nils Smith, illustrates how this assumption can be misleading.[15] At twenty-five months Amahl consistently pronounced *puddle* as *puggle*. At the same time, however, *puzzle* came out as *puddle*, so it was certainly not the case that Amahl could not say the word. At a later stage Amahl systematically replaced *s* by *th* when it began a word. So he pronounced the word *sick* as *thick*. But at the same time he substituted *f* when he was aiming at *th*, so when he tried to say *thick* it came out as *fick*. The crucial determinants of what the child says seem to be what he is aiming at and his regular patterns of producing those sounds. The child progresses by closing the gap between what he says and what he means to say.

3/Words

A child's first fifty words typically include the names of the salient objects or events in his world. Important persons like Mummy, Daddy and Granny; favourite foods like bananas, biscuits and juice; and such highlights of the daily routine as baths and poohs – these are the focus of the child's attention. Children also soon learn the names of common animals like dogs, cats, cows, horses and pigs, together with the noises they make. In urban societies these animal words are often learned from picture books or toys, but children transfer them immediately to the live animals. Other early words in a child's vocabulary, at least in English-speaking Western societies, include words used to effect a change in his environment or to regulate his interaction with his parents – *ta, more, no, up, out, open*, and the like.

A striking aspect of many children's early vocabulary development is the way they overextend a word to refer to objects that lie outside its normal range of application for adults. For example, a child might use the word *doggy* to refer not only to all dogs but also to cows, horses, sheep and cats. The overextension of a particular word may last for some months, but often it occurs only briefly before the child learns the correct names of the objects. Furthermore, the child may overextend only some of his words; others will be used appropriately from the beginning.

The list of overextensions reproduced here is taken from early diary studies in which linguists kept a record of children's words and the first referents of those words.

Child's word	First referent	Extensions	Possible common property
bird	sparrows	cows, dogs, cats, any moving animal	movement
mooi	moon	cakes, round marks on window, round shapes in books, tooling on leather book covers, postmarks, letter O	shape
fly	fly	specks of dirt, dust, all small insects, his own toes, crumbs, small toad	size
koko	cockerel crowing	tunes played on a violin, piano, accordion, phonograph, all music, merry-go-round	sound
wau-wau	dogs	all animals, toy dog, soft slippers, picture of old man in furs	texture

In many cases it seems that the child has identified the meaning of the word with only one property of the object:

its shape or sound or size. He then uses the word to refer to all objects sharing that property. As the child learns more words, he adds other defining properties to his word meanings to distinguish them from one another. When a child who overextends *doggy* to all four-legged creatures comes to learn the word *cow*, he may add to the property of four-leggedness the requirement that things called *cow* be relatively large and things called *doggy* relatively small.[1]

In the examples listed here all of the referents of a particular word share a single property. In many other cases, however, the child seems to extract not just one but several attributes of the objects to which adults apply the word. He then extends the word in his own speech to other objects that share any one of those attributes. Nicholas provided us with an amusing example of this kind of over-extension. At a year he learned to call our hairy dog by her name, *Nunu* (a Zulu word meaning approximately 'little wild beast'). He immediately used that word for all dogs, real or pictured. Before long he began to use it to refer to any animal or bird and at the same time extended it to other furry objects, such as slippers and coats. He even said it while cuddling a warm blanket. But the most exotic overextension occurred when we took him to a restaurant when he was thirteen months old. When the salads arrived they were topped off with pitted black olives. These suddenly caught Nicholas's eye. Pointing a stubby little finger at them he said 'Nunu' and proceeded to pick them up and eat them. For a moment we were puzzled, but suddenly realized the similarity between Nunu's nose and shiny black olives.

Similar overextensions occur in children's early use of verbs. As in the case of nouns, the child seems to have a best referent for the word, usually the action most fre-quently named by the parents. But he then extends the word to any action that shares some attribute with that best referent. Thus, one little girl learned the word *kick* at the age of seventeen months and used it first and most consistently for the action of propelling an object forward with the foot. But during the next three months she applied it to many actions that bore a similarity to kicking. She said *kick* while watching turtles doing the can-can in a television cartoon, watching a moth fluttering on the table, just before throwing something, and when she bumped a ball with the front wheel of her kiddy car.[2]

What kinds of similarity among objects and events underlie the child's early use of words? Frequently the objects share some perceptual property such as shape, size or sound, but a word can also serve to name objects with a similar function. Thus all objects that a child puts on his head, regardless of their shape or size, may be called *hat*. Nicholas first learned the word *narna* for bananas, then used it to refer to bananas, apples and oranges, and later called everything that he could eat *narna*. Even more abstract properties are also extracted by the child from his experiences and used as a basis for categories to which he applies a word. Some children use the word *heavy* to refer to all situations involving physical exertion with an object, regardless of whether it is heavy or not. In each of these cases the child forms a category of objects, events, or experiences with some property or set of properties linking them together.

For most overextensions it is not that the child confuses the objects and therefore calls them all by the same name. A child who calls all round objects *apple* can usually still pick out the apple from a set of other round objects such as oranges, balls, and rings. In comprehending the word the child uses all of the properties of apples that he knows – apples are the round, red, and sweet-tasting fruits that are good to eat. In his production of speech, on the other hand, in his desire to communicate or draw the adult's attention to an object, the child will use the word in his vocabulary that best fits the object, even if he knows it is not quite right. Children may even use overextension as a strategy for discovering the names of objects, since parents typically supply the correct word when their child over-extends a word to an inappropriate object.

Finally, the child might be drawing an explicit comparison when using a word in this way; Nicholas's use of *Nunu* for the olives may have meant *like Nunu*. Some overextensions might therefore represent the earliest signs of metaphoric usage in children's speech. As a criterion for saying that a child intends a word to be taken metaphorically, we usually require that the child should have an option between using the literal or the metaphorical description of the object, and Nicholas certainly did not know the word *olive*. But another example from Nicholas illustrates how tempting it is to ascribe to him at least the basis for metaphorical comparison. By fifteen months Nicholas had divided the animal kingdom into four categories: *Nunu* (dogs and other small animals), *moo* (cows and other large animals), *du* (ducks and other birds), and *turtle* (turtles and other toys that swam in his bath). *Turtle* was overextended in typical fashion to a variety of objects that shared some property, perceptual or functional, with the original toy turtle. It generalized first to other toy turtles, including one with wheels, to real turtles, and to pictured turtles. But several other objects were then called *turtle*: a picture of a multicoloured corncob; other toys that swam in his bath, including a walrus and a wind-up frog; and a pine cone with a stem that stuck out like a turtle's head. The most metaphorical overextension came when Nicholas was riding along in the back of our car wearing his all-in-one pyjama suit. The suit was much worn and frayed at the feet, and Nicholas's big toe protruded through a hole in one foot. Suddenly he lifted his foot in the air and said delightedly: 'Turtle!' In his over-extensions the child is overlooking a large number of dissimilarities between the objects and drawing attention to their similarity along some other dimension. This is a crucial aspect of our use of metaphor. The power of a metaphor seems to lie in the unexpectedness of the dimension of similarity and the way in which it captures the essence of the object being described in metaphorical terms.

Whereas the overextensions of words are most noticeable in early language, children also underextend some words. The word *animal* is typically applied only to mammals at first. Two-year-olds will deny that some birds, fish and insects are animals or that people can also be called animals. In this sense the range of application of some early words needs to be narrowed down, but the meaning of other words needs to be expanded in the child's vocabulary development.

Objects can be named at different levels of generality. A rose can be called *Constance Spry*, a *rose*, a *flower*, a *plant*, a *living thing*, or an *entity*, depending on the information that one wishes to convey. Children first learn and apply words for objects at an intermediate level of generality, and only later learn their more specific names or the general categories into which they fall.[3] So a child will typically learn the word *flower* before he separates *roses* from *daffodils* and *tulips* and before he can call flowers, trees and grass *plants*. In part this is the result of adults' naming practices. Parents name things differently for two-year-olds than they would for adults. A mother who would name coins *nickels* and *dimes* for an adult will call them all *money* for her child. Cars will be identified as *Volvos* and *Datsuns* for an adult but as *cars* for the child. There is a practical reason for this, though we are not always conscious of it. The level of specificity at which objects are named corresponds to the level at which those objects require the same action from the child.[4] The two-year-old has no need to distinguish between *roses* and *tulips*; he need only know that those objects that are to be smelled and admired, but not eaten or trodden on, are all *flowers*. Grouping all *plants* together under one name would be too general for those purposes, since the young child will be encouraged to trample and roll on some plants (grass) and cajoled into eating others (lettuce). Similarly, the round, flat objects that adults value and that can be exchanged for candy and other goods, but must not be swallowed or thrown away, are all *money*. Only when he goes to the store on his own does the child really need to distinguish between coin denominations. The child's mental grouping of objects that are behaviourally equivalent may be as influential as the naming practices of parents in determining the way in which he uses early words. So even if he hears and learns more specific or more general adult words for objects, he will use them to name sets of objects that require similar behaviour from him. Nicholas first learned the word *penny* for cents, but he immediately used it for all coins. When he later learned the word *money* it simply replaced *penny* in his speech. All coins became *money*, the name we called them, and *penny* actually disappeared from his speech for a while.

There is an intricate relation between the child's classification of objects into categories and his learning of word meaning. Sometimes he will already have classed a set of objects together because they look similar or because he has been taught to treat them all in the same way. Then he simply has to learn which word applies to that whole category. But he may still make over- or underextension errors if he thinks the word applies to only some part of his category of objects, or if he thinks it includes a broader range of objects than those he has classed together. The two-year-old's use of *animal* provides an example of this kind of underextension: he may know that people share many properties with other animals, breathing, sleeping, and eating like them, but he has to learn that they can be called both *people* and *animal*. At other times the way that adults use a word may actually lead the child to classify objects in a new way, either subdividing a category he has already formed or broadening the category to include more objects. Nicholas's use of *penny* is a case in point: he had to learn that *penny* referred only to the little copper coins, not to the silver ones.

THE FUNCTION OF THE
FIRST WORDS

Many of the early single-word sentences of children do not serve merely to label or to point out objects, but are used in the service of social interaction. Some children may use words for one function more than the other, leading to differences in the words they learn. Some children are primarily *referential*, learning and using words that label objects. At the other extreme are *expressive* children, who first learn words for personal desires or for aspects of social interaction; words like *bye-bye*, *want*, *naughty* and *more*. The referential-expressive dimension is clearly a continuum, and most children have both types of words in their early vocabulary, but the classification reflects the predominant use to which the child puts language in the one-word stage. To some extent the child's early use of language reflects his mother's verbal style. Mothers who spend most of their time pointing out objects and their properties tend to have referential children; mothers who use language mainly to direct their child's behaviour tend to have expressive children.[5]

Whatever early words the child learns, he soon uses them to communicate a variety of things. A given single-word utterance can greet, label, demand, or query some object or state of affairs, or it may even deny the truth of an earlier statement by the parent. At the beginning the child accompanies the single word with gestures, pointing or grasping at the object; later he varies his intonation to signal the different meanings of the utterance. Most commonly a rising intonation indicates a query and a falling pitch marks a statement, but some children adopt idiosyncratic intonation patterns that have no clear counterpart in the adult language. Still other children will not employ consistent intonation patterns until they are combining two or more words into sentences.[6]

Speech gradually plays a more and more important role in the communication between parent and child, but it comes into an established rich network of nonverbal communication, and at first it may even be redundant. Many of the more basic rules of conversation seem to be set before the child ever produces words. For example, people have to take turns at speaking, recognize their turn to speak, and not dominate the exchange. The roots of these conventions may lie in the ritualized turn-making games of parent and child – like peek-a-boo or build-and-bash (where the parent builds and the infant bashes). It is in this nonverbal discourse with the parent that the infant first learns to use eye contact to establish and maintain interaction, and looking away to terminate it. Similarly, the precursors to shared linguistic reference may lie in the developing ability of the infant to follow his mother's gaze to an object, followed by his development of pointing. In short, the one-year-old child is quite adept at regulating nonverbal discourse with people he knows well.[7]

The case of autistic children provides a stark contrast to the normal development of nonverbal communication between parent and child. Autism is a disorder that strikes early in childhood and distorts many aspects of the child's development. Most characteristic of severely autistic children is their almost total withdrawal from social interaction. They treat people like inanimate objects, making little or no eye contact. At most they may manipulate the other person's arms or hands as if they were playthings. This lack of interest in others led to the term 'autism' – a preoccupation with oneself. Social withdrawal may show itself within the first year, when the infant is peculiarly unresponsive to the mother. He may not develop a smile in response to others and constantly resists being picked up or cuddled. He may make no response to his mother's comings and goings, being unusually content when left alone. Later, autistic children often develop sudden and irrational fears (of a particular toy or colour, say) and have severe tantrums or spells of inconsolable crying for no clear reason. Many of them indulge in repetitive motor behaviour like rocking back and forth in a chair for hours or twisting the hands about in front of the eyes. Their behaviour may even become self-destructive, with the child rhythmically striking his head or arm against an object, apparently oblivious to the pain. In the light of our discussion of the importance of social interaction as a precursor of language, it is significant that autistic children, the classic case of social withdrawal, typically show severely disordered language acquisition.

The normal eighteen-month-old often seems to understand far more of the speech he hears than his own utterances would lead one to expect. To some extent this is because his comprehension of words, intonation and grammar usually precedes his spontaneous use of them. But in comprehension he also has available to him far more information than the speech alone provides. Parents' speech to little children refers to familiar objects and events that are usually present at the time of the interaction, and it is accompanied by elaborate gestures. The child uses his knowledge of the events being mentioned, what is likely in that situation and what his parents expect of him, as well as his understanding of the words that are used. When the child speaks, although he can manage only a word or two at a time, parents use their knowledge of the context and the events that led up to the child's utterance to interpret it, so there is little loss of communication. In this way the child communicates much more by a single-word utterance than the word itself, successfully requesting objects or information, drawing the adults' attention to an object or event, or initiating a familiar game. At this stage, then, he need not possess a great deal of linguistic sophistication to communicate with adults in situations where words are redundant in context.

4/Rules

Extensive vocabulary is an impressive hallmark of human language, but it is not sufficient to express all the ideas we wish to convey. Admittedly we can often express ourselves well with a single word and a lot of elaborate gesturing if there is support from the context, but imagine trying to get a message across over a telephone, a high fence, or in writing if word meaning were all that we had. We would need a new word to express each relationship into which an object might enter, and clearly such a language would be hopelessly inefficient and difficult to learn. Instead, languages have a grammar, a system of rules that govern how words can combine to make sentences. None of us is taught these rules explicitly; as children we learn them by listening to the speech of others and gradually piecing together the recurring regularities. Once the grammar is learned, we are capable of making new sentences to cover any conceivable situation.

Imagine a child trying to tell his mother that he has just observed a car and a truck in collision, and it was the truck's fault. He might have all the component words, 'bump', 'truck' and 'car', and could repeat each of them several times, but his mother would have to guess which vehicle caused the accident. A child who has learned the rule that, in English, the agent (or initiator of the action) is expressed before the action, has a substantial advantage in communication. He could say 'truck bump' or 'bump car', or the ultimately informative 'truck bump car'. Word order, then, is one common means of elaborating upon the information contained in the words themselves. By arranging words in orders agreed upon by the language community, the child can go beyond the words alone to express the relationships holding between them.

What kind of relationships can be expressed in English by word order? As mentioned, one such is the identification of the agent of an action versus the thing affected by that action. Another is the direction of possession, as in 'my father's mother' as opposed to 'my mother's father'. Yet another is the locational relation between objects: 'the box is on the chair' as opposed to 'the chair is on the box'.

When young children first begin to combine words, usually at the age of eighteen months to two years, their combinations are not random. They are in fact less likely to say 'eat Daddy' than 'Daddy eat'; 'coat Mommy' is not as likely as 'Mommy coat'. Children seem to select from all possible orders just those that are used by adults to describe a particular relationship. So when word combinations first appear, children are sensitive to the adult conventions for ordering words in sentences, and in English these are the earliest rules of grammar they learn.

English-speaking children express a limited range of meanings in their first sentences. They talk about actions, what happened to what and who does what:

> Me fall.
> Bump table.
> Car go vroom!

They are concerned, not to say obsessed, with the relationship of possession:

> My teddy.

Mommy hat.
Daddy hair.

Equally prevalent is the relationship of location:

Cup in box.
Car garage.
Mommy outside.

Among other early meanings that find frequent expression
at this stage are recurrence:

More milk.
Tickle again.

nomination, or labelling:

That Teddy.
This steamroller.

and nonexistence:

Beads all gone.
No more soup.

Comparatively rare in the earliest word combinations, but
still occasionally expressed, are relations involving experiences that are not actions:

See that.
Listen clock.

and relations involving states:

Have coat.
Daddy [is a] policeman.

Children learning many different languages, among them Samoan, German, French, Hebrew, Luo (in Kenya), and Russian, seem to encode the same limited set of meanings in their first sentences.[1] This lends credence to the notion that the meanings depend on, and are restricted by, the two-year-old's understanding of the world. At this age he has recently begun to understand what causes some things to occur and to remember which person initiated an action; he spends his days figuring out what objects he is allowed to touch and which he is not; and he occupies many hours filling holes and experimenting with what will fit in any container he can get his hands on. Of course, he also keeps track of where the important people and toys in his life are at any moment.

His language therefore reflects his knowledge of the world, but it may also help to increase or at least refine that knowledge. The direction of effect between language and thought is a deep philosophical question, but it can be raised even about these humble beginnings. Take an example involving one of the relationships expressed very early: possession. Some languages, like English, express all the multitude of possessive relationships with word order and the possessive 's marker on the first noun. So, for example, *great-grandmother's silver teapot* is expressed in the same way as *Mommy's dress*, although great-grandmother may no longer be seen in association with her teapot. Similarly, *Daddy's chair*, called that because of occasional use but consistent preference, is expressed in the same way as *Daddy's shoes*, which are almost always in contact with Daddy but removed to go up to bed, unlike *Daddy's nose*. Other languages have different means of expressing these varying relationships. Some languages mark the distinction between common associates like *chair*, and nonremovable parts of the body like *nose*. Every child can learn any human language, but he cannot know in advance of learning it how broad or narrow his concept of possession must be to accommodate the rules of his language. It is by hearing other people talk that he learns that some of the multitude of distinctions he can make are relevant to his language, and others must go without expression. So it is not that language simply takes over an existing system of knowledge. Instead, each language draws attention to alternative ways of encoding events, enhancing the similarity of some relationships and contrasting others. Whether this has any profound effect on the way people from different cultures see the world is a matter of dispute. It is likely that language borrows from, but does not exhaust, the set of ideas that can occur to people.

To determine what the child really knows, it is necessary to record a very large sample of his speech, usually about 500 sentences. Children often produce complex sentences borrowed wholesale from the speech of others, and their parents see this as typical of what their child can say at that age. Although not denying that they often represent prodigious feats of memory for one so young, it is wrong to take these borrowed sentences as representative of the child's knowledge if he shows no sign of creating his own sentences after that model. It is rather like an adult claiming to be a poet because he has memorized Coleridge's *The Ancient Mariner*. It is composition, not production, that is the critical feature of both types of language use. Sentences that are reproduced without being composed have been called prefabricated routines, and some examples in the early stages are *what's that*, *what's this*, *howdoyoudo*, and a curious one from a linguist's young son, *matteroffact*!

Retarded children begin to combine words into sentences at a later age than usual, so it is possible that the meanings they express might reflect their longer experience with the world. As it happens, however, their language is almost exactly like that of a normal child of the same *mental* age, where this is assessed by comparing their motor skills, memory and so forth. The same limited set of meanings is expressed in their first sentences, though the rate of development is much slower. Two children aged four and six who had IQs of around 50 made the same progress in one year that a normal child makes in one month at a much earlier age.[2] The only marked difference in the speech of these two children compared to normal two-year-olds was the fact that the retarded children used many more prefabricated routines than is usual, seemingly relying more on rote memory than on building novel sentences. It is not certain that this is a real difference in the language learning of retarded children, however, for it might be that the process is so stretched out that routines which have only brief lives in a normal child's repertoire become the central feature of the slower child's language.

In most children these rather rigid formulas give way to a system of rules that is remarkable for its flexibility: an infinite number of new sentences can be composed despite a finite vocabulary. In order to discover the regularities of composition, a child must be able to segment the stream of speech he hears into its component units. Technology has revealed how incredible this process is, though most of us would guess it to be trivial. Contrary to popular opinion, there are no real pauses between words, and there are no consistent breaks at phrase or sentence boundaries. In fact, speech is easy to segment only when one already knows the units. The child must learn by keeping track of the recurring segments in the speech he hears and constantly updating his guesses about the language and its rules, a process made considerably easier by the fact that language is spoken in context.

As mentioned in Chapter 3, a pervasive characteristic of autistic children is a problem with language. In particular, autistic children seem to have problems with the detection of patterns or regularities in the world around them, and this would severely hamper their language learning. Some autistic children may perceive sentences as long words because they are unable to break them down into their components and understand that they are composed of smaller, meaningful units. Such a child may learn a stock of sentences rather like a tourist phrase book, which he will use whenever a situation recurs that is somewhat like the one in which he first heard it. Once, for example, an autistic child was banging his feet against the wall next to his bed when he was supposed to be napping, and his mother called threateningly to him, 'Do you want me to take your shoes off?' From that moment he used this entire sentence whenever he was in a situation with the same emotional overtones of misbehaviour and threatened punishment. Other autistic children, particularly those confined to institutions that employ the passive medium of television as entertainment, have a repertoire of word-perfect advertising jingles. The jingles are repetitive, catchy, highly predictable, and thus represent a more stable and undemanding linguistic input than anything else in the child's world. A ward full of such children is a sad thing to experience.

How does a normal child discover the units that make up sentences? He is aided at first by the fact that most adults begin by speaking very simply to children. In some cases they use single words when the child is starting to learn language. So the child begins by recognizing some words as wholes before they ever appear in combination. On the other hand, certain elements of language are never spoken in isolation but are always attached to other words, for example, the tense endings *-ing* and *-ed* in English. Why is it necessary to detach them from the words to which they are joined? One argument would be that it is a clumsy way to learn a language, to have to store in memory all the various forms of each verb: *carry, carries, carrying, carried*. However, a more compelling reason is that we can hear a new word and understand its potential uses. We hear a sentence such as 'He can larate very well' and we can go on to produce 'He is larating', 'He larated', and so on, showing that we have available the elements *-ing* and *-ed* to combine with any new verbs we happen to hear.

In children's speech there are two aspects to the process of identifying morphemes, which are the smallest units of meaning. All words are morphemes, as are the plural *-s*, the past tense *-ed*, and the comparative *-er*, since these convey additional meaning. In some cases children wrongly segment the speech they hear so that the units are too large. Adam, a child intensively studied by Roger Brown, produced sentences such as *it's raining, it's cold, it's funny,* but went on to say *it's went, it's was working,* and demonstrating that he had not correctly separated *it* from the morpheme *'s* that frequently attaches to it. A second common error is when children correctly segment the morphemes but are then overzealous in their use of them, producing such conspicuous mistakes as *holded, falled, foots, sheeps.* If the English language were perfectly regular these would be good constructions, but it is not and it contains exceptions that have to be individually committed to memory.

Grammatical morphemes are the next addition to the English-speaking child's language. Typically their function is to subtly modulate the meanings of sentences. The child learns to mark tense by adding *-ing* or *-ed*; the prepositions *in* and *on* to distinguish different kinds of location; the articles *a* and *the* to distinguish between definite and indefinite referents; the possessive *'s* and the plural *-s*. The manner in which children acquire these morphemes has been thoroughly documented, and several findings have emerged. First, when a child learns a morpheme, say the past tense *-ed*, he does not learn it for all verbs at the same time. At the beginning he uses it most reliably on verbs that denote activities that can be completed, such as *dropped, closed* and *jumped,* but less often on verbs naming activities that have no clear end, such as *talked, watched, walked.* The process is thus piecemeal; only gradually does the child use the past tense for every verb in the way an adult would use it. The child takes time to learn all the conditions of a morpheme's use.[3]

A second finding that has attracted attention is that there is a consistent order of mastery of the most common morphemes. In other words, the plural -*s* and the progressive -*ing* on verbs are almost always the first to appear, followed by the prepositions *in* and *on*, the articles *a* and *the*, and only much later by the forms of *be* such as *is*, *was*, *were*, *are*. The agreement among children is remarkable, and the order of difficulty appears to be a function of the linguistic complexity of the forms rather than their frequency. To use the plural requires a sense of number, to use a past tense requires a sense of 'earlierness', but one needs to know *both* number and tense to choose appropriately among the forms of *be* – should it be *is* or *are*, *is* or *was*? The forms of *be* are therefore more complex and are acquired later than the plural and the past tense.

In terms of comprehension, children are aware surprisingly early of the extremely subtle meanings that the morphemes carry. In one recent study, girls of seventeen months of age were shown a new doll-like creature, and one group was told 'This is zav', another group, 'This is *a* zav'. Then they were shown similar dolls among other toys. The first group called only the original doll *zav*; similar dolls were not called *zav*. The second group called all the similar dolls *zav*. So the first group treated *zav* as a proper noun; the second treated it as a common noun, although the only clue to this difference was the presence or absence of the article *a*. Long before they used articles in their own speech, these children were sensitive to the meanings they carry.[4]

In another experimental study, three-year-old children were shown pictures containing three unknowns: for example, a man using a strange tool to perform some novel action on some strange substance. The experimenter then talked about the picture, saying either 'Here is *a* sib', 'Here is *some* sib', or '*Here is sibbing*'. In adult language *a sib* would be a unique entity, *some sib* would be a mass substance, like snow or spaghetti, and *sibbing* would be an action. The morphemes provide the only clue to what is being labelled. To find out what the children thought was being described, the experimenter presented them with three new pictures, one showing only the tool, a second only the substance, a third the action. The three-year-olds were reasonably adept at selecting the correct picture: they chose the tool if told 'a sib', the substance if they had heard 'some sib', and the action if told 'sibbing'.[5] Thus they could use the morphemes as clues to the likely referent of a totally new word. This must be of considerable help to the child in discovering new meanings in the speech around him.

EARLY SENTENCES

To give some idea of how fast the child's progress in grammar can be, compare the columns in the list below.

Eve at eighteen months	*Eve at twenty-seven months*
More grapejuice.	This not better.
Door.	See, this one better but this not better.
Right down.	
Mommy soup.	There some cream.
Eating.	Put in you coffee.
Mommy celery?	I go get a pencil 'n' write.
No celery.	Put my pencil in there.
Oh drop a celery.	Don't stand on my ice-cubes!
Open toybox.	They was in the refrigerator, cooking.
Oh horsie stuck.	
Mommy read.	I put them in the refrigerator to freeze.
No Mommy read.	

Write a paper.
Write a pencil.
My pencil.
Mommy.
Mommy head?
Look at dollie.
Head.
What doing, Mommy?
Drink juice.

'An I want to take off my hat.
That why Jacky comed.
We're going to make a make
a blue house.
You come help us.
You make a blue one for me.
How 'bout another eggnog
instead of cheese sandwich?
I have a fingernail.
And you have a fingernail.
Just like Mommy has, and
David has, and Sara has.
What is that on the table?

The sentences on the left were spoken when this child was less than two years old, and those on the right were said by the same child nine months later. Of course the grammar is not perfect, but her sentences are much more complex. The changes do not reside only in the addition of grammatical morphenes, but also in the elaboration of different parts of the sentence and the appearance of well-formed questions and negatives.

One striking development occurs in the child's ability to express all the components of a sentence. In the early stages, he may omit the subject or produce several sentences in a row, alternating what he mentions:

Daddy truck.
Get truck.
Truck, Daddy.

Apparently unable to produce more than two words at a time within one sentence at this point, he relies on stringing sentences closely together so that one can serve as the context for the next. This is evident when the child uses a word like *put*, which requires specification of an agent, an object, and a location. It is insufficient to say, with one element unspecified,

John put dish.
Put in refrigerator.

Yet young children do this frequently, relying on previous utterances or gestures to fill in the missing part. During the age range of two to four years, children improve dramatically in being able to say everything in one sentence.

Around this time the child also learns to expand single nouns into noun phrases. Groups of words are used to make referents more specific:

Dog.
That dog.
That brown dog.
That brown dog of Mr Smith's.
That brown dog of Mr Smith's that ran away.

The child first learns rules for combining words; those rules now have to allow for combining the larger phrases. In theory we can expand any noun into a noun phrase that can be incredibly long, and can use that complex phrase in any position in the sentence. Just as words can occupy different positions in sentences depending upon their relationship, so can whole phrases. So we can say either

I saw *that brown dog of Mr Smith's.*

where the phrase is the object, or

That brown dog of Mr Smith's is a pest.

where it is the subject of the sentence. The building blocks of language are highly flexible.

Children begin making sentences with simple noun phrases, and at the start they are not particularly flexible. The subjects of the first sentences are often pronouns, such as *it*, *that* or *he*, whereas the objects tend to be simple nouns. But object noun phrases are the first to become elaborated, and there is quite a delay before subject noun phrases are made more complex. There are two possible reasons for this. Subjects of sentences tend to be *given* information, whereas the predicate tends to be *new* information. There is not much point in elaborating something that is already understood, so the child is not likely to say 'my new red truck dumped the toys out' because his listener already knows which truck is being talked about. A second reason may be that it is easier to produce complexity at the end of a sentence. Even adults go off track when the subject is too elaborate, and the main verb seems lost for ever:

That man you were telling me about that you met in that little hotel in Spain the year before you went to Paris rang you last night.

Although the child has complex noun phrases in certain positions, he does not use them in other places in the sentence – which suggests that children do not yet share the flexibility of the equivalent adult forms, or of single words. The first elaborations are the addition of adjectives to nouns, usually one at a time unless the child uses them for emphasis. One two-year-old got so excited while talking to us that she surprised even herself with the following sentence:

You can't pick up a big big kitty 'cos a big big kitty might bite!

Verbs also become increasingly elaborate until they too are multiword phrases. The first elaboration comes with the tense markers mentioned previously; then shortly afterwards the auxiliaries – *can, do, will, may* – are added to verbs. Usually the first, and most overused, of these additions are the 'words' *gonna, hafta* and *wanna*, which are learned as wholes and only later recognized as *going to, have to* and *want to*, perhaps not until the child tries to write them.

In the third year, then, the structure of sentences is extremely simple: both noun phrases and verb phrases consist of one or two words. Joining sentences together is quite rare. However, the child is also learning at this stage to express in a conventional way the negative and interrogative form of sentences. It is not that the child does not say no or ask questions before this. They appear in the one-word stage, but the child does not know the grammatical expressions that adults use.

Negatives

The child's first negatives consist of the words *no* and *not*, which are simply tagged on to his simple sentences.[6] There are a number of different functions subsumed under the negative in English, though other languages separate them by different forms. A child can deny something:

That's not yours!

He can reject something:

Not that one!

He can comment on its nonexistence:

Hey, no pocket!

The underlying similarity in the functions of the negative seems to be a discrepancy between a belief or wish and a state of affairs, and that discrepancy has to be present before one can make a negative statement. There are always hundreds of things that are not true, but we are forbidden by the laws of communication from expressing them, unless someone believes otherwise. We cannot go around saying, however truthfully, 'You don't have three heads', or 'The ceiling isn't purple', or 'That dress you're wearing isn't mine'. Instead we have to wait until someone either declares the reverse or acts as if the reverse were true. From a surprisingly early age, children are sensitive to that unwritten law and seem to understand the conditions under which one can and cannot produce a negative statement.

Despite limited means of expression, then, children understand and use the fundamental aspects of negation almost from the start. They progress by adding the more conventional aspects of the language, first by learning the negative auxiliaries *won't*, *can't* and *don't*. These appear before the corresponding positive forms *will*, *can* and *do*, making it likely that the negative forms are learned as wholes, not as constructions of *will+not*, *can+not* and *do+not*. By the age of three or four, however, children usually have a whole range of auxiliaries, both positive and negative: *would/wouldn't*, *was/wasn't*, *has/hasn't*, and others, and at this point it seems likely that they can relate the positive and negative forms to each other. At least they can play the game described in Chapter 1 where one puppet is induced to argue against another, showing that they can negate just about any auxiliary offered:

He must buy socks.   He mustn't buy socks.
The big dog will bite you.   The big dog won't bite you.

It is many years before they master the use of the negative with indefinites such as *some, none* and *any*. The following sentences from an older child illustrate the complexities of those rules:

> I didn't see nothing.
> Nobody can have some supper.
> Don't let someone touch this.

Questions

The child's first questions are typically signalled by rising intonation, with the words in their normal sentence order:

> I have some?
> You like dis?

Occasionally, when the auxiliary first appears, it does not occur at the beginning of the sentence as it would in an adult question, but in the middle:

> We can go home?
> You will bath me?

This has suggested to some researchers that in making a question we begin with a statement and then move the auxiliary to the front.[7] The children who produced the preceding sentences had not learned that rule. It is difficult to prove this because the mental steps people go through in producing sentences are inaccessible. It does seem, however, that negatives and questions are more difficult constructions than statements, and making a negative question such as:

> Wasn't he there?

is yet more difficult, both for adults to understand and for children to produce. Negative questions are extremely rare in children's speech.

Other types of questions the child learns to express in the third year are *wh*-questions – *where, what, when, who, why* and *which* – and the question *how*. The child's first such question is inevitably some variant of *whatsat* – *whassat, whatsit, whaddis, whatisdis*. At the age of eleven months Nicholas picked up *whatisdat* as one of his first 'words' and pronounced it very accurately. We were trying in vain to keep him under control in a restaurant when he lunged over a neighbouring diner's shoulder and demanded loudly, 'Whatisdat?' to which the startled woman answered: 'Fish!' The form is learned as a whole and it is some time before it becomes productive, that is, before one hears the variations that are the sign of true composition: *what is dat, what are dese, what is it doing*. Like the other questions, the *wh*-question requires the auxiliary to be placed before the subject, but many children go through a stage where they position it after the subject just as in a statement.[8]

Where we can go?
Why he must do that?

Notice that this is the order of words required when the question is embedded in another sentence:

I don't know where we can go.
He told you why he must do that.

One Japanese child learning English as a second language at the age of five years decided at one stage to double up on the auxiliary as a safe strategy.[9] Some of her sentences were:

You will see where is your house is.
I don't know where is the telephone number is.
I don't know where is the woods is.

The different *wh*-words all stand for different parts of the sentence, and thus answers to them reveal how much children know about the different components of a sentence. The *wh*-questions are similar in form, but the answers to them are diverse:

What is he climbing?	He is climbing *the ladder.*
Who is climbing?	*The boy* is climbing.
Which boy is climbing?	The *red-haired boy* is climbing.
When is he climbing?	He is climbing *after lunch.*
Where is he climbing?	He is climbing *on to the roof.*
How is he climbing?	He is climbing *very easily.*
Why is he climbing?	He is climbing *to rescue the cat.*

Children can only answer those questions that require components of a sentence they use readily. So children begin by answering *what, who* and *where* questions quite well, since this is the kind of information – agents, objects and locations – that their own sentences can express. However, they do not yet understand the notions of manner, causation, purpose, or time, and they are apt to answer questions that relate to those notions as if they were familiar questions. Young children often give wrong answers to some *wh*-questions:

When are you having lunch?	In the kitchen.
Why are you eating that?	It's an apple.

In fact, the ideas that underlie *why* questions are so complex that children must take some time to sort out the appropriate answer. They also ask *why* questions of the most exasperating kind because they do not understand the conditions of their use. Parents can get trapped into answering impossible questions, which is fortunate in the long run because the child can only work out what *why* questions mean by studying them in conversation. One child's progress in learning about *why* was followed over time.[10] At around eighteen months of age the little girl asked *why* following a negative statement from an adult. But she did not seem to know if the answer was what she expected:

Adult: The cat has a body but no head.
Child: Why?
Adult: Why? I don't know why. Did somebody break it?
Child: (no reaction).

By twenty-six months, she attached *why* to phrases taken from the adult's statement, making her questions even more perplexing:

Adult: That's the garage door.
Child: Why the garage door?

At this stage if *she* were asked a *why* question, she admitted, 'I don't know.' A couple of months later she had attached *why* not just to phrases but to whole propositions, which is a little bit closer to the adult form, though the conditions of use were still as broad and unfocused:

Adult: He's reading a book.
Child: Why he reading a book?

Now, at least, the adult could offer some reasonable

answers and display to the child some of the varieties of explanation that languages contain. But the child still did not understand these explanations and merely offered some aspect of the situation in reply:

Child: I can't wash this.
Adult: Why not?
Child: In here.

For the development of understanding, then, a child must be witness to a large number of conversations that include *why* questions and answers. He cannot know in advance of this experience when it is appropriate to ask *why* or what constitutes an acceptable answer.

It is important in this discussion of questions not to neglect their function in conversation, quite apart from their structure (for example, where the auxiliary must be placed) or their meaning (what they refer to). The question form is used for a wide variety of purposes in adulthood, only some of which relate to finding out missing information. They can serve as comments on another's behaviour, and leave little room for reply:

Why do you insist on wearing that awful tie?

Or as polite forms of requests for action:

Would you mind removing your feet from the table?
How many times do I have to tell you to get those tadpoles out of my sink?

Perhaps the intonation, or the look on the mother's face as she speaks, gives these forms away, since even at the beginning few children mistake them for true questions. A common kind of question to ask children is when the adult already knows the answer. The speaker uses the question to check out the child's knowledge, or to display it for someone else:

What colour's this?
What were you going to tell Grandma about your party?

Interestingly these 'false' questions are in abundance in speech addressed to very young children, and they would seem to play an important role. The adult already knows the answer so he can provide corrections to the child's answers; if he lacked the information and asked a true question, he would not know whether to believe the child's reply. Only when adults have gauged the state of the child's understanding do they trust him to answer genuine questions.

Learning words is not all there is to language. The child soon learns rules to combine words to make sentences, and adds the subtleties of tense, plurals and articles. He learns the adult ways to make negatives and questions in all their variety. The progress towards adult grammar is not flawless, and the errors the child makes provide a glimpse of his emerging system of rules.

5/Relationships

It is difficult to characterize the major change in language skills that takes place in the later preschool years. More words are added to the child's vocabulary, his sentences become longer and he becomes a better conversationalist. But underlying these advances is a more profound change: the child now appreciates relationships. Conventional wisdom tells us that a word 'stands for' something, that we should be able to point to an example to convey the meaning. But this procedure is seriously inadequate for many terms in a language. The word *big*, for example, does not refer to some particular size, but varies with the object described. A big spoon, a big kitchen, a big city – what makes the term appropriate is the relationship between one object and others of its kind. Children must understand that relationship before they can use the adjective appropriately. Other words shift meaning not with the physical context but with the conversational circumstances: the word *I* refers to the speaker, *you* to the hearer, so that paradoxically a child is always called *you* but must never call himself that.

Even in his earliest sentences a child shows that he is uniting different parts of a situation into a relationship, rather than labelling them one at a time. Language relates more than words, however, and a major development in the later preschool and early school years comes in the child's attempts to relate sentences to one another so that he can express the relationship between entire events. Each sentence is no longer an isolated entity, and the child becomes more proficient at discourse. He can now assimilate information from the context as a whole: the relationship between objects, between speaker and hearer, between one event and another, and between present and preceding dialogue. These relationships unite the accomplishments of the period of three to six years and form the topic of this chapter.

RELATIONAL WORDS

The spatial adjectives, *big/little*, *tall/short*, *thick/thin*, and so on, provide one of the best examples of words that are not fixed in meaning but vary with the objects described. The first of this set to appear in the child's speech are the terms *big* and *little*, which occur quite early and are used for a wide variety of objects. The child of three seems adept at knowing whether a particular shoe is big or little with respect to shoes in general, the same being true of other familiar objects such as balls, pins, or chairs. If given an unfamiliar object, he will sensibly fall back on comparing the object to himself as the standard: perhaps, if he can easily handle it, it is called *small*, but if it cannot be picked up it is *big*. So the child proceeds by learning about particular objects, and he extends that knowledge to new cases in reasonable ways.

The other spatial terms emerge only later in the child's spontaneous speech, and tests reveal some uncertainty about their use. A child of three may be unsure about whether *tall* refers to the height or the width of an object. He may know that it means larger in some respect, but not which dimension it refers to. Given two stick figures that vary in height, he will be accurate at pointing out the *tall* one. However, if the stick figures vary in width as well as height, he may get mixed up. The same is true of terms like *thick/thin*, *fat/skinny*, *wide/narrow* and *deep/shallow*. The child learns first that they are opposites, and then which dimension is referred to by each pair.[1]

The child's knowledge of opposites between the ages of three and six can be illustrated by the entertaining language game using puppets. The child is introduced to a particularly contrary puppet who says 'just the opposite' of what a second puppet says. After models of opposites have been given by the puppets, the child is asked if he would like to operate the contrary puppet. The adult's puppet then says a word and the child's puppet has to produce its opposite. Children's errors on this game are quite revealing of their knowledge of spatial adjectives. Young children can give *big* as the opposite of *little* and vice versa without any hesitation, but if they are given a word like *tall* they often say *little* or even *skinny* rather than *short* as its opposite. At this stage they seem to know that the terms refer to size and can often correctly identify which end of the scale is being referred to; but they cannot always specify the dimension that the adjective pairs describe.[2]

On the opposites game and tests of the child's comprehension of spatial adjectives, the adjective pairs are consistently ordered in terms of their relative difficulty.[3] *Big/little* is the earliest pair to be mastered, followed by *tall/short* and *long/short*, which are in turn easier than *wide/narrow* and *thick/thin*. *Deep/shallow* is particularly difficult, giving pause even to five- and six-year-olds. The order of difficulty of these terms for the three-year-old seems to be determined by two factors. One is the frequency of the adjectives in speech. *Big* and *little* are by far the most frequent in the speech of adults and children, and we talk about the relative height and length of objects more often than their width or thickness. But *big* and *little* are also more general terms than the others and so are easier to use appropriately. *Big/little* refers to size along any spatial dimension as well as to the combination of the dimensions. *Tall/short* and *long/short*, on the other hand, specify a particular dimension along which size is to be measured. Finally, if we look at the specific dimensions, height and length appear to have psychological primacy and be more salient than width or thickness. We usually describe an object in terms of its height and length before its width or thickness – a table is 'six feet long and three feet wide', a door is 'seven feet high and thirty inches wide', a man is 'tall and thin'.

In learning all of these spatial adjectives it again appears that children first accumulate individual examples of what *tall*, *wide*, or *deep* mean for particular objects, so they are not always able to use them appropriately for new objects. A child might learn which end of the swimming pool is *deep* and which is *shallow*, but not understand how to apply those terms to holes or sinks or rivers. In some situations, then, it will look as if he understands the terms as well as an adult, but his knowledge of the words will in fact be restricted to familiar objects.

Words like *here/there*, *this/that* and *my/your* also have no fixed referent but vary with the speaker as well as the context. For example, if someone is working on a jigsaw puzzle he might talk of *this* piece *here* versus *that* piece *there* when the pieces are only inches apart from each other and very close to the speaker. In contrast, someone walking around a city might say 'shall we go to *this* café or *that* café' when both are distant and neither one in reach. It probably takes children several years to learn how the terms shift with the size of the context, and some begin by using *this* for things in reach and *that* for things out of reach. However, they must also master the shift in reference from speaker to hearer. When a child says 'Where's my ball?' and his mother replies 'Over here', he will fail to find it if he looks around himself, although he would call that location 'here' if he spoke.

Children first master this shift in reference for *I* and *you*, *my* and *your*, probably because those terms do not also involve consideration of the size of the context. *I*, *me* and *my* refer to the speaker, *you* and *your* to the hearer, regardless of context or topic of conversation. It is curious that normal children have so little difficulty in learning the correct use of the pronouns *I* and *you*; yet those terms constitute a major stumbling block for children with autism. Autistic children frequently reverse *I* and *you* – a child says 'You got hurt' as he jerks his hand away from a hot stove, or 'You want some juice' when he clearly means 'I want some juice'. Some normal two-year-olds also refer to themselves as *you*, but in normal development this is a very brief stage. In contrast, autistic children persist in the *I/you* confusion and most never resolve it.

If much of the autistic child's speech consists of echoes of the sentences he hears, as we suggested earlier, then it is understandable that he should call himself *you*, because others call him that. However, such a child may also say *he* or *she* when *you* is the appropriate pronoun, suggesting that he does not merely reverse pronouns because he echoes speech but because he is confused about the role of interactors in a conversation. He fails to distinguish persons in verbal interaction with him (*you*) from others in the situation (*he/she*). It is not clear whether this is due to a lack of self-identity – the child has no integrated concept of his own self as distinct from others – or a general failure to understand complex relationships that are expressed in language.

By the age of three most normal children can not only understand the distinction between *I/you* and *my/your*, but they can correctly choose which of two cups is *this* one versus *that* one and which cup is *here* versus *there* in the following situation:[4]

The child and adult sit opposite each other across a low

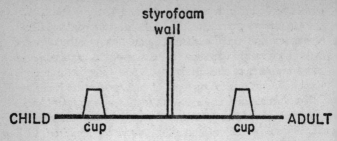

wall that separates two upturned cups. The child closes his eyes while a candy or a raisin is hidden under one of the cups, and he is then told 'it's under *that* cup' or 'it's over *here*' by the adult, emphasizing the terms *here/there*, *this/that* and *my/your*. The three-year-old is reasonably correct in this situation, and can usually also inform the adult correctly using these words when it is the adult's turn to find the hidden prize. In different circumstances, especially when there is no dividing barrier, children of five or six still have difficulty choosing the correct cup.[5] Mastery of the terms is therefore at first restricted to situations in which there is a clear physical reference point, such as the wall.

RELATING PROPOSITIONS

In the last chapter we described how the young child begins to express the relationship that holds between words, rather than producing a string of single words. He becomes able to code in language the difference between *dog bite man* and *man bite dog*, among other things. A grammar does not stop at rules for relating words, however; it also has means of expressing the relationship between whole propositions or events. Consider the two events: *the comedian joked about the actress*, and *the actress hit the producer.* Think of the myriad number of ways that those propositions could relate. They could simply have *and* between them, which would make the order of events and their relationship relatively ambiguous. If *then* is added, however, there is no doubt as to the order:

The comedian joked about the actress; then the actress hit the producer.

If the link word is *because*, the sentence expresses a different temporal order and gives information about the motive for the first event:

The comedian joked about the actress because she hit the producer.

The relationship changes again if the link is *but*:

The comedian joked about the actress but the actress hit the producer.

Children begin by talking about events in isolation from each other, but from the age of three or so they often join sentences by *and*, which is an all-purpose conjunction that does not require specification of the relationship in detail. It is ambiguous with respect to order, motivation and so on. Much later they use the other conjunctions – *but*, *because*, *while*, *however*, *if . . . then*, and the like. Usually they will know a few routines that include them, but they are not very good at generalizing their use to new situations.

Children use strategies of one kind and another to help them solve the meaning of long sentences they hear. One strategy is to assume that the order in which events are mentioned is the order in which the events took place. If a three-year-old child hears:

After you clean your teeth, brush your hair.

or

Clean your teeth before you brush your hair.

he will probably perform the acts in the right order. However, if he instead hears the opposite order of mention:

Before you clean your teeth, brush your hair.
Clean your teeth after you brush your hair.

he will tend to do the things in the order in which they are mentioned, neglecting the information carried by *before* and *after*. Children do not understand the true meaning of these conjunctions until they are much older.[6]

Joining whole sentences with a single word is only one of the ways that languages combine sentences to express relationships. Another way is by embedding one sentence in another, as in relative clauses. For instance, the two sentences:

The boy hit the woman.
The woman carried a stick.

can be combined in various ways depending upon the topic of interest.

The boy hit the woman who carried a stick.

makes the second sentence a relative clause of the first, so it is now embedded in the first sentence. Alternatively, the first sentence could become the relative clause:

The woman that the boy hit carried a stick.

Children and adults find it more difficult to understand sentences in which the embedded sentence occurs in the middle than when it occurs at the end.[7] They tend to go astray if they have to hold the subject of the main sentence in memory for too long. This is especially true if some other interpretation immediately presents itself. So from the sentence:

The deer that kicked the man chased the boy.

the child is likely to extract the sentence:

The man chased the boy.

which is not an event that occurred. Both adults and children try to assign grammatical roles to words as they hear them spoken, in keeping with their knowledge of how sentences are typically constructed. It is this tendency that allows us to understand speech so rapidly in normal circumstances, but it can lead us astray, as when we try to read the headline:

'Delays Dog Deaf-Mute Murder Trial.'

Comprehending the relationship between sentences takes some years to master, but what about sentence production? The process of how children begin to relate propositions into single sentences has been studied in children's storytelling, where children are asked to repeat a story they have been told. Children of two or three are rather poor at conveying the relationship between the events in the story. They tend to speak single sentences or link them loosely with *and*, and they do not necessarily maintain the order of events.[8] The first relative-clause constructions to appear are routines such as those for beginning stories:

There was this cat *called Fred.*
There was a princess *who lived in a golden palace.*

Typically the first productive, that is, not stereotyped, relative clauses occur at the ends of sentences, which is in keeping with the child's better understanding of those forms. However, true relative clauses are not common in children's speech until school age, and expressing them in written form takes considerable time to master. In fact, much of the research on older children's language has come from teachers of English in the schools.

PASSIVE SENTENCES

The grammar the child learns between three and six has to do with expressing the relationships between propositions and also with the relationship of an event to the context of discourse. For instance, the passive voice

The boat was spotted by the helicopter crew.
The man was bitten by the dog.
The girl was rescued by the coast guard.

rearranges the normal order of agent and object (the thing affected by the action), and is used when the object rather than the agent is the focus of attention or interest. The above sentences would be appropriate if the boat, the man, or the girl were more important to the speakers than the helicopter crew, the dog, and the coast guard.

Children do not understand passive sentences well until the age of four or five or even later. Two- or three-year-olds respond to most passive sentences by randomly choosing either noun as the agent. But their comprehension varies with the plausibility of the alternative interpretations of the sentences. Even young children have no trouble interpreting:

The candy is eaten by the girl.

since there is only one thing the sentence could mean. Interpretation of other sentences depends upon the child's understanding of which of the two alternatives is more likely, as in:

The dog is patted by the boy.

It is unlikely, but not impossible, that the dog pats the boy, and some young children will opt for that alternative. Most tests of children's acquisition of the passive voice use sentences that contain no clues to meaning other than those carried by the order of the words and the presence of *by*. In these reversible sentences the events are more equally likely, so the child must understand the passive voice to act them out appropriately. Some examples are:

The cow is kicked by the horse.
The rat is bitten by the cat.
The girl is kissed by the boy.

To deal with reversible passive sentences, many three- and four-year-olds assume that the first noun is the agent, which is true of the more common declarative sentences.[9] On hearing:

The cow is kicked by the horse.

children treat it as if it meant

The cow kicked the horse.

In testing one child we presented her with the passive:

The truck is bumped by the car.

and she took the truck and bumped the car. We then told her:

Now make the truck bump the car.

She gave us a withering glance and said, 'Again?' It was clear that she had heard the two sentences as exactly the same and thought we were being repetitious.

By five or six years children can understand some passive sentences, but still not all of them. For example, they learn what passives mean when they contain action verbs such as:

The mouse was bitten by the squirrel.

but not when the verbs do not refer to actions:

The man was remembered by the boy.[10]

Children have particular difficulty with the verb *follow*, as in:

The cow is followed by the horse.

Interestingly, the equivalent passive sentence in French and German gives children learning those languages the same amount of trouble.[11]

In virtually all these tests of children's acquisition of the passive, however, sentences are presented out of context, so that the normal motivation for drawing attention to the object is missing. Comprehension is much improved if the object is made the focus of attention. For instance, in one study children who did not understand the passive were told a story containing appropriately motivated passives.[12] The hero might be a small frog and various things happen to him:

The frog was frightened by the tractor.
The frog was helped by a sparrow.

After hearing the story the children showed improved comprehension of other passive sentences.

In this chapter we have surveyed a number of developments in the child's expression of relationships, ranging from the relationship between objects that must be appreciated in order to use certain adjectives correctly to the relationship between events and the context of conversation. There are a couple of general lessons to extract about how the child learns language. The first is that learning is often not independent of context so that showing that the child knows something about one word or one situation does not mean that he will know it if the situation changes even slightly. A child might know the meaning of the word *deep* with respect to swimming pools but not baths; he might understand the word *here* when the situation involves facing someone across a barrier but make mistakes if the barrier is removed; he may understand passive sentences with some verbs but not others. The rules of reference and of language that we know as adults are a great deal more abstract than the child's knowledge. The general rules emerge for him only later on, after he ties together all the particular pieces of information he has learned in specific situations.

The second lesson has to do with the relation between comprehension and production. It is usually the case that children understand some aspect of language before they produce it, but that observation requires two qualifications. Some children speak without really understanding, as when a child has a routine phrase that he has parroted but knows only the most superficial conditions of its use. A child might know that to begin a story you say 'Once upon a time', or, like one four-year-old living in an academic household, learn that you can break into conversations by saying: 'I read an article.' Also, the conditions of testing production and comprehension must be the same in order to compare them, since we know that the child can have peculiar islands of accuracy amid a sea of confusion. For instance, a child might be producing correct passive sentences with action verbs like *kick* or *throw*, but fail if asked to understand passive sentences with verbs like *know* or *remember*. Even more important, the supporting cues must be the same in each case. Parents tend to use elaborate nonverbal signals to help their children understand instructions, so that in these natural circumstances it is difficult to tell how much the language is contributing to the child's response. An adult instructing a child to pick up a toy will usually point at it, look at the child, and then glance at the toy, and change intonation as the child makes successive approximations to the right response, rather like saying 'warm . . . hot . . . hotter!' in hide-and-seek. Under such conditions, comprehension is bound to look more proficient than production. When the circumstances are more fairly matched, the production and comprehension abilities of the child are remarkably similar and seem governed by the same principles. Finally, comprehension is much better in contexts that approximate the situations in which those particular grammatical forms are naturally used.

6/Freedom of Speech

The language of the child begins as primitive behaviour; it serves only a limited set of purposes and is tied to the immediate circumstances of its use. By contrast, reflecting on language as a system of symbols and their relationships is the preoccupation of linguists, philosophers, and cross-word-puzzle fanatics. How does language as a communicative act become language as an object of contemplation? The years from three to six hold the key to this remarkable advance.

Consider the skills the child must learn to become a mature language user. First, an adult speaker does not only talk about events in his immediate experience – events are remembered, predicted, or conjured up from imagination. He describes events remote from himself in space and time, bringing them second-hand into the experience of his listener. This characteristic of language makes possible the transmission of human culture from one generation to the next, so that each child need not repeat the experiences that gave rise to that culture.

Second, in conversation the speaker must know what referents, implications, and presuppositions are shared by his listener, and what must be fully specified. When talking to close friends or in the presence of the events that form the topic of conversation, the speaker can use elliptical language that relies heavily on contextual support. He can say, 'Look what it's doing now' or 'He'll fall' or 'Where did you put my thingamajig?' and be perfectly understood. On other occasions, however, the speaker must recognize that his knowledge is not the same as his listener's and must establish all the important unknowns.

Third, a mature speaker (and even more so a writer) can act as his own audience, trying out different effects, constructing puns, detecting ambiguities, and correcting grammar. He possesses the ability to think about language and treat words and statements as if they were objects. These three skills – a freedom from the here-and-now, the ability to take account of variations in shared knowledge, and an awareness of language forms – all distinguish the language of adults from the early language of the child and from the natural communication systems of animals.

EXPANDING CONTEXTS

In the earliest stages of development the child's speech is very much tied to the here-and-now. There is little or no reference to the past and none to the future, and no talk of hypothetical events, so there is little to indicate that the child can do without the support of the immediate context of his utterances. In a short while, however, the child begins to refer more frequently to things that are not physically present. At first he might only have produced the words *more milk* upon seeing the bottle, but later he will tug at the refrigerator door or ask for it while playing in the garden. The words have become detached from their original stimulus and the child can now request objects in their absence. Around the same time the child demonstrates that he remembers things that happened in the past, though at first only people who know him well will understand his oblique references to past events. A child with only single words may come to a flight of steps where he has fallen and say 'boom', reliving a painful memory. By two and a half or three, the typical child will have enough language structure to use tense markers or adverbs of time that indicate even to strangers that the event took place in the past.

References to the future take a little longer to appear, and parents soon learn not to promise treats in the distant future, for a tiny child hears nothing but the mention of a treat and not the fact that it will take place 'tomorrow' or 'after we have supper'. By the age of three, however, children are usually beginning to talk of future plans, although this future may be immediate, tied to what they are presently doing: 'I'm gonna tie this here', 'I'm gonna go ride my bike', and so forth.

An understanding of the future may be one component skill required to make hypothetical statements, sentences that refer to possible outcomes contingent upon some other event:

If you stick this in here then it should go better.
If it rains we'll go to the movies.

However, there is more to the hypothetical than a sophisticated understanding of time relationships: it also involves assessment of likely outcomes, and this depends on a broad knowledge of the world, of people and their motives, and of cause-and-effect conditions. The grammar of the hypothetical in English is complicated, and it does not appear until around four or five years.[1] Although in Russian the grammar involved is elementary, the hypothetical still is not used until late in the preschool years because so much in the way of intellectual development is requisite to its use.[2]

The child begins to speak bound by circumstances; he ends by using language to invent circumstances. This freedom from the immediate situation manifests itself in another way in the child's imaginative play. The first words are usually spoken in the presence of the objects or actions that they name. It is possibly more true to say that we demand this as part of the evidence that our children have 'real' words, for if a child of ten months says *car* perfectly when no car is around, we are likely to dismiss it as babble. As we have seen, children progress to extend their earliest words to objects bearing only partial resemblance to the original or most common referent, but there is another, parallel, development. The child is learning that certain changes in an object do not change its name: two-dimensional pictures of dogs are still *dog*, tiny plastic cars are still called *car*. At about eighteen months to two years, the child embarks on a form of play that is called *symbolic* because it makes one object stand for another in the way that words stand for objects. A toddler might pick up a matchbox and move it along a bench, saying 'vroom, vroom!' Or he might take a thimble and pretend to drink from it. In each case he knows what the object really is, but he conceives of a playful use for it. At first, the role of language is debatable. Frequently we use the child's speech to read his intentions in his imaginative play, and some people have argued that both speech and symbolic play derive from a common root in the child's intelligence.[3] However, before long, new possibilities are awakened by language. The child can say to his playmate, 'Let's pretend we're aeroplanes', or 'S'pose this is a tent and we're lost in the woods'. The situations are enriched by a language no longer tied to the here-and-now, and this growing freedom is characteristic of the first six years of life and beyond.

As the child's words and sentences become further and further separated from the situations they describe, it is as if the child now carries the context of language around with him. In the early stages of language development the burden of communication is carried by the child's partner in conversation. The adult listener uses all the knowledge at his disposal to guess at the child's intention, and this involves using the situation as a cue. Imagine a scenario in which a one-year-old is looking at a beautiful blue balloon on a shelf. He might gesture wildly in that direction and say 'ba! ba!' and a co-operative adult can guess without too much difficulty what he wants. Within a short time the child will be able to ask for it when the situation is quite different. Perhaps he will be reminded of it as he looks through a picture book, and will demand it from his listener, saying 'ba!' If he is fortunate, his listener will be the same person as before and will realize what he wants. However, as the child's social life expands, it is quite likely that the listener will not be the same and will not have witnessed the original incident. Unless the child develops the further skill of being able to take into account his listener's knowledge, and make the necessary adjustments to the information he communicates, the fact that *he* carries the context with him and can relive it will be for nought.

SHARING KNOWLEDGE

Children have been called egocentric, literally self-centred, because they expect others to share their knowledge and point of view. In a test where they have to communicate a very specific message to someone else behind a screen, they are notoriously bad even at seven or eight years.[4] Imagine two six-year-olds separated by a screen, each having in front of him an array of pictures. The first child is supposed to tell the second which picture he has selected. The following dialogue is typical:

First child, pointing to a picture in front of him: 'It's this one.'

Second child, pointing to a picture from his set: 'You
mean this one?'

First child, unable to see, answers confidently: 'Yep.'

Certain early linguistic skills can provide a window on
how the child begins to take into account his listener's
perspective and knowledge. One example is the contrast
between the definite and the indefinite articles of English.
The conditions of correct use for the articles are quite
subtle and complex, but we shall focus here on the way
their use shifts with the listener's state of knowledge. If a
speaker and his listener both know what is being referred
to, then the speaker can use the definite article *the*. One
of us can say to the other, for example:

Have you walked the dog?

and be understood, there being only one dog in our life.
However, if only one of us has a particular dog in mind,
he cannot use the definite article without first cre ʳ g
shared knowledge. There are many ways to do this, perhaps
the simplest being to describe it first:

I was walking home when I saw *a* huge Alsatian. I
passed an open gate and *the* dog nearly took my leg off
at the ankle.

When it is first mentioned, the indefinite article is used,
but thereafter, because it is common knowledge, it can be
called *the dog*.

Young children of two-and-a-half to three-and-a-half
years are already sensitive to this rule of discourse in certain situations, and usually use the definite article when
knowledge is shared. But a common error is for them to
assume shared knowledge when it does not exist, so they

overuse the definite article for the first mention of an object.[5] A child might run into a room and ask:

Where is the picture?

without allowing for the fact that not everyone knows the particular one he has in mind. A difficult lesson that the child learns over the first ten or more years of life is that others do not have the same privileged access that he does to his thoughts and past experience, and that to be skilful in conversation he must share that knowledge explicitly.

AWARENESS

The final advance we shall describe is the change in the child's awareness of language. Children learn language as a medium of communication, but as it becomes less and less bound by circumstances and more and more flexible, its properties seem to become available for conscious inspection. Language becomes an object of awareness instead of a transparent vehicle of meaning. This can be shown for all the different levels of language: sounds, words and grammar.

It is very hard for most children under the age of five to understand that words are made up of separate sounds. Questions such as 'What is the first sound in your name?' or 'If you take the *s* sound off *scream*, what's left?' leave young children mystified.[6] Words are distinguished in speaking and understanding by means of these small sound differences, but it is quite another matter for children to talk about those sounds. Curiously, children who talk to themselves in their cots (a common phenomenon) spend a great deal of time playing with the sounds of language, experimenting with different pronunciations.[7] It is paradoxical that they are unable to bring those playful skills to bear on the task of reflecting about sounds. It may be that the cot-talker is building up his skill bit by bit, and if the researcher could choose examples from the child's practised repertoire, even a young child might be more proficient at answering such questions.

When do children know what a word is? They use words in everyday commerce from an average age of eighteen months and yet have great difficulty in talking *about* words. One early observation was that children tended to believe that words are mystically connected to the things they name – a cat, for instance, *has* to be called *cat*; it would be unthinkable to call it anything else. Children who learn two languages from an early age recognize more quickly that words are conventions, and a cat can be called just about anything as long as people agree about it. A different confusion occurs in asking children to give examples of words. Even at four or five years of age, most children confuse the word with the thing it names. So if a child were asked 'Is *car* a real word?' he will happily concur, perhaps adding, 'You can drive it.' If the questioner asks instead, 'Is *is* a real word?' the same child would say, 'No, it's not anything.' Gradually over the age range of four to seven years, children begin to give as a definition of a word the statement 'Words are what you say' or 'You talk with words', but they have difficulty sticking to that definition when called upon to judge words. Despite their claim that words are part of the language rather than the world of objects, they nevertheless deny that *is*, *very* or *but* are words, because 'you can't see them' or 'they're not real things'. If asked 'Tell me a long word', such children might suggest 'snake' or 'string', confusing word and object. One inspired child covered all her bets with the answer: 'Empire State Building'. It is surprisingly late, around eight years, that many children can begin to talk of words as part of the language and can free the idea of a word from its referent.[8]

Awareness of grammatical rules is also a late skill that can be traced over this age range. It is possible to play a puppet game with co-operative children aged two-and-a-half years and older, in which they are induced to teach a puppet how to talk properly.[9] The introduction goes as follows: 'This puppet has an awful problem. He doesn't know how to talk. He says things all the wrong way round. Can you listen and see if you can help him?' The adult then asks the puppet to say some things, and the puppet speaks either correct or reversed sentences, for example, 'Teeth your brush'. The adult then says, 'That's wrong! You say *Brush your teeth*. That's the way to say it.' After the child has heard five or six models, some right and some wrong, he is encouraged to participate and his judgements are informative. There seem to be several stages to the child's awareness of sentence 'goodness'. At first, he either responds at random or accepts all sentences as 'right', even those that reverse the correct order of words. Yet it is not that he cannot play the game, because at the same time he will consistently reject any sentences that violate sense. If he hears a sentence like 'Tickle the table' or 'Throw the sky', he vigorously objects to it.

When children first judge the correctness of the sentences, they cannot offer suggestions for corrections, and it is difficult to know on what basis they judged a sentence to be 'wrong'. When corrections do appear, they at first seem to involve considerations of meaning. A child will say 'No! Not *House a build – Live in a house*, that's what he should say.' Increasingly, however, his corrections of wrong sentences retain the original words and meaning of the reversed imperatives and correct only the word order. By the age of four years he can ignore the message and pay attention to the form, at least in this very simple situation.

Subtler aspects of language, such as those involved in

ambiguity, are at the root of much verbal humour, but children are not aware of them at first. Language contains a great many ambiguities that rarely enter our awareness. Words themselves can be ambiguous because of the way they are pronounced – *bored/board* – or because there are two meanings for a single word, say, *watch*. Sentences can be ambiguous because they allow two or more readings.

The shooting of the hunters was terrible.

can mean either that the hunters were shot or that they did the shooting. In another kind of sentence ambiguity, small differences in intonation or pausing allow us to distinguish two meanings, but the written version is ambiguous.

He fed her dog biscuits.

could mean either that he fed biscuits to her dog or dog biscuits to her. In everyday conversation or reading we often do not notice ambiguities because the rest of the conversation, or the context, leaves no doubt as to which meaning is the right one. Only when we can suspend the influence of context and pluck out a word or a sentence from its normal communicative purpose can we reflect upon it and see the alternative meanings. This ability to see two meanings at once is exploited in many jokes and riddles.

It stands to reason that if a child cannot reflect on language, he will fail to appreciate ambiguity. One way to test this idea is to show children a set of pictures and ask them to choose the ones that show, for example,

The eating of the chicken is sloppy.

If the child sees the potential ambiguity, he should pick out both a picture of a chicken eating and a picture of someone eating chicken. It is not until third grade that most children succeed at this task.[10]

If young children fail to notice ambiguity, then why do they laugh at jokes and verbal riddles? It turns out that they often laugh for the wrong reason. Their lack of comprehension of a joke can be shown in two ways: paraphrase and explanation.[11] If a young child is told a joke and then is asked to repeat it, the chances are good that he will paraphrase the meaning in his own words, as he would do with an ordinary message. In the case of jokes and riddles, the words have been chosen very precisely to create some kind of double meaning. On retelling it, the child invariably wrecks the joke. For instance, a child is told the following:

Why is the man in the fish market stingy?
Because his job makes him sell fish (selfish).

He is likely to retell it as follows:

Why is the man in the fish market stingy?
Because he sells fish.

In rephrasing it, the joke has evaporated.

At the same time that children recall jokes in this faulty way, they show no real preference for riddles over non-riddles. First-year schoolchildren do not prefer riddles such as:

What do giraffes have that no other animals have? Baby giraffes.

to nonriddles:

What do giraffes have that no other animals have? Long necks.

It is as if they do not see the distinction between ordinary language, for communicating messages, and play with language as in jokes and riddles. They do, however, realize that jokes are socially valuable, and try very hard to use words to make people laugh. Sometimes a child will learn a stock joke format but have no conception of what makes for a good answer. Four- and five-year-olds mistakenly believe that they, too, are clever enough to make up jokes.

If young children are asked to explain what is funny about a joke, their answers reveal that they do not really know. The ability to recall a joke verbatim seems to go hand in hand with an awareness of where the humour lies. A joke told to two second-graders goes as follows:

How do you keep fish from smelling? Cut off their noses.

The boys revealed divergent talents in their explanations of the joke:

Dirk: It means smelling like sniffing instead of smelling like stinking.

Peter: Because if you cut off their nose, and everything smells with their nose, they can't smell because they have no nose. It's funny . . . because I don't think fish really have noses.

Peter's response is typical of younger children: he has not grasped the notion that language itself can be humorous but believes instead that jokes must describe humorous situations. Even in the early school years, then, the medium of language is still a transparent one. Language is for conveying messages, and its form has not fully entered conscious awareness.

Flexibility of language use and awareness of language forms also characterize the skilled reader and writer. A reader must understand language without the benefit of nonverbal cues to meaning, gestures, or support from an environmental context; a writer must use language that best conveys the meaning he intends, taking into consideration that the reader's perspective may well be different from his own. Reading requires the awareness that words are separable from their referents and can be represented by written symbols. Finally, for a child to learn an alphabetic or syllabic writing system he must realize that words are made up of smaller sound units.

Do the language skills we have described promote literacy, or does literacy promote them? Must we wait until a child has mastered them before we try to teach him to read? From three to six years these aspects of language are acquired without explicit instruction, though the process of mastery continues into the school years and may be influenced by exposure to written language. What remains to be determined is how many children who have reading difficulties also suffer from deficiencies in discourse skills and awareness of language forms. If these abilities form an essential foundation for good reading, the questions become: what experiences are critical for their development, and what environments might facilitate their emergence? We do not yet have answers to these questions.

7/Crucial Experiences

We have now answered the easiest of the three questions posed at the beginning of the book. In the first chapter we outlined the methods employed by psychologists and linguists to study children's language, and in subsequent chapters we described the stages that children typically go through in their progressive mastery of adult pronunciation, grammar, word meaning, and conversational skills. In describing the pattern of language development, however, we have occasionally referred to the physical and intellectual maturity of the child or the nature of the language he hears from his parents as factors determining that pattern. It is to those and other possible determinants of language acquisition that we now turn in order to answer the hardest question: how does the child learn language? How do his experiences, social and linguistic, shape his language learning, and what, if any, are the limitations on the rate and pattern of learning?

THE CONTEXT OF LANGUAGE ACQUISITION

As we have stressed throughout the book, the child does not learn to speak in isolation from other people, as if he were listening to a radio or tape recorder. Language acquisition normally takes place in the context of a rich interaction between the child and his parents. Several facets of that interaction seem to be important facilitators of language acquisition, and some of them may even be necessary for the acquisition of normal speech.

Parent-child interactions in the first year set up a wealth of shared knowledge and expectations, and may also establish in the child some of the precursors of reference and conversational skills. The child begins to use gestures and direction of gaze to draw attention to an object, and learns to interpret the corresponding adult gestures. He comes to understand when a response is required of him and when it is not – in familiar situations and games he even learns what response is expected from him. Since most of the early conversations between parent and child take place in familiar contexts and concern objects that are present in the situation, the child already has a good idea of what the parents' sentences are about. This simplifies the child's task of relating the adults' words and sentences to the objects and events they describe.

The quality of the language that children hear from their parents and the way in which it relates to their own comprehension and production of speech may also be important factors in language learning. Listening to the speech of adults to one another leads one to wonder how the child ever learns to speak properly, let alone so quickly. Speech between adults is not only grammatically complex; it is also surprisingly ungrammatical. Sentences run into each other or are interrupted and often incomplete. Sometimes they assume a great deal of knowledge on the part of the listener. If the child has to learn language from this kind of degraded input, the process of acquisition is something of a mystery, and some early linguists therefore concluded that the child must come to the task with considerable inborn knowledge of language. Recently, however, studies have shown that parents' speech to young children differs in many important respects from their speech to adults.[1] Mothers (and fathers too, although they have not been studied as much) tailor the length and complexity of their utterances to the linguistic ability of their children. Mothers' speech to one- and two-year-olds consists of simple, grammatically correct, short sentences that refer to concrete objects and events. There are few references to the past and almost none to the future. Sentence intonation and stress are greatly exaggerated, and clear pauses appear between sentences. Furthermore, as many as 30 per cent of the utterances are repetitions, partial or complete, of one of the earlier sentences of the mother or the child. These general properties characterize the speech that the child might hear from many people, not just his mother. Adults, whether or not they are parents, simplify their speech to young children in similar ways. Even four-year-olds speak more simply, concretely, and slowly to two-year-olds than they do to adults. This means that even in non-Western societies in which older siblings provide a great deal of the child care, the young child receives a simplified language input. Finally, similarities far outweigh differences in mothers' speech to children across the different social classes and cultural groups that have been studied.

What determines the characteristic properties of speech to children? Different properties seem to depend on different factors. The less developed the child's comprehension of speech, the shorter and simpler his mother's utterances are and the more she repeats herself. To some extent this is controlled by the child as well as by the adult. Signs of noncomprehension by a child lead at once to a reduction in the length of the utterances of the adult talking to him.[2] In other situations where we are striving to be understood, such as when speaking to foreigners, we also shorten our utterances and make them grammatically less complex. We use more concrete nouns and verbs, and fewer grammatical function words, just as we do with young children whose understanding of speech is suspect. Other features of speech to children, such as the use of a higher-pitched voice and special babytalk words containing simplified speech sounds, reflect the adult's conception of the way children talk. The adult assumes that the young child finds certain sounds and words easier to pronounce than others. Interestingly, a higher pitch and the use of special words characterize speech to pets and the language of lovers as well as babytalk, perhaps as a sign of endearment carried over from our language to children.

Finally, some properties of speech to children of different ages seem to depend on what the parent is trying to do with language. With a child of one or two years the mother is often trying to manage and direct the child's behaviour, as well as provide him with the names of objects. So the mother's speech is full of imperatives and sentences that name or identify a person or object. To older children, on the other hand, the mother is far more likely to address requests for information and statements that provide the child with more information about his world. Attempts to get the child to do something are now likely to be couched in the more polite indirect question form: 'Why don't you put your toys away?' or 'Could you please stop interrupting Granny?' rather than in the blunt imperative. In this way the relative frequency of different sentence types in parental speech changes as the child gets older.[3]

How might the speech modifications made by adults assist the child in learning language? The restriction of early conversations to familiar settings and to objects and events that are present in those situations greatly simplifies the child's problem of learning the words for things. It limits the range of possible referents for any new word and provides the child with clues from the situation that might indicate what is being referred to; clues such as the speaker's direction of gaze or the presence of a new object among familiar ones. Adults also use recurrent sentence frames in talking to children: 'Look at the ———', 'That's a ———', or 'Where's the ———?' The word that enters into the frame is usually heavily stressed, so the child's attention is drawn to it. In this way new words are introduced in familiar sentence contexts. The high pitch of the adult's voice and her exaggerated intonation and stress indicate to the child that he is being addressed, and also emphasize the important elements of the sentences. Since young children tend to imitate the stressed elements in sentences, the exaggeration of the sentence stress may enhance this process of acquiring words. Finally, adults usually supply names for objects at an intermediate level of generality. Roses, tulips and chrysanthemums are all called *flowers*; coins all become *money*. This corresponds to the level at which the child might naturally have grouped those objects already, since it is the level at which the objects require similar behaviour from him.

Other features of mother-to-child speech may help the child to divide speech up into words, phrases, and sentences. Single-word utterances are quite frequent, and even multiword sentences are slowly enunciated and have distinct pauses between them. Mothers also tend to repeat isolated phrases and words following the complete utterance. A mother might say: 'Put the red truck in the box now. The red truck. No, the red truck. In the box. The red truck in the box.' In addition to making it clear to the child what he is required to do, the mother is isolating the component phrases of the sentence. This lesson in the structure of sentences is reinforced by a common type of question asked of young children, the so-called *occasional question*, in which the *wh*-word does not occupy its usual initial position in the sentence, but occupies instead the position of the element that is queried. These questions might ask the child to repeat a phrase from his previous sentence:

Child: Wanna cookie.
Mother: You want what?
Child: A cookie.

or require him to elaborate a word or phrase:

Child: I ate it.
Mother: You ate what?
Child: The candy.

In other interactions the mother might prompt the child by recasting her question:

Mother: Where did you put it?
Child: (no answer)
Mother: You put it where?

Such recastings of *wh*-questions help to reveal the structure of the question form in English. Children are actually more likely to answer occasional questions like those above than they are to answer a regular *wh*-question, perhaps because they more emphatically require an answer or possibly because they are easier for the child to understand.[4]

Nevertheless, it has proved difficult to determine which of the modifications in adults' speech to children are really necessary for normal language acquisition, or even if any of them facilitates the child's learning of language. Could a child learn to speak just as well by listening to adults talk to one another or by watching television? Ethical considerations clearly preclude us from any experimental tests of these questions which might involve isolating children from verbal interactions with other people, but naturalistic observations have provided at least a partial answer to some of the questions about the importance of adult-to-child speech. In one research project a group of Dutch children whose interactions with their parents were being studied happened to watch a great deal of German television. Yet they did not acquire any German words or grammar from this exposure.[5]

Other researchers studied a normally hearing child, Jim, whose parents were both profoundly deaf.[6] The parents had only a few words of oral speech and used sign language to each other, but they knew that Jim could hear so they thought it inappropriate to use sign language with him. He therefore saw adults sign to each other but had only rudimentary gestures directed towards him by his parents. Under these conditions he learned no formal sign language, just a few gestures. Jim had little contact with other children or speaking adults but he watched television frequently, so most of the language he heard came from television programmes. He heard only the occasional single-word utterance from his parents. Jim was two and a half before he tried to use language, at which point he produced a few words, most of them taken from television jingles. At the age of three years and nine months he came to the attention of speech therapists and researchers, and his language skills were extensively tested. Jim fell well below his age level on standard tests of linguistic ability, and in several respects his language differed from that of children with normal language development. The intonation patterns of his utterances were abnormally flat, communicating little affect. Although he tried to communicate concepts appropriate to the situation he was talking about, he lacked the necessary knowledge of English grammar, so his sentences possessed a very idiosyncratic structure. This is apparent from the sentences shown in the list below.

Speech of a normal child of deaf parents
at three years, nine months

1. House. Two house. Not one house. That two house.
2. Not window. Two window.
3. That enough two wing.

4. Two crayon. Big two crayon.
5. My mommy my house a play ball.
6. My mommy in the house apple.
7. House chimney. My house my chimney.
8. Fall that back.
9. Be down go.
10. There crash it.
11. That car it go truck.
12. Go downstairs snack.
13. Off my mittens.
14. Not broke that.
15. This not take off plane.
16. Right there wheels.
17. Going house a fire truck.
18. Where is it plane.

The first four examples demonstrate that Jim had formed the concept of plurality but he had not learned the regular plural marker -*s*, although it is among the first grammatical morphemes mastered in the normal acquisition of English. The last seven examples suggest that Jim had created some of his own rules of sentence production: they all consist of a phrase followed by a specification of the topic of that phrase. This is the opposite of the word order typically used in English by both adults and children.

Fortunately, Jim's story has a happy ending. After regular therapy sessions, Jim showed dramatic improvement in his speech. In one month he progressed a full year in age level on standard tests, and at four years and two months his mastery of English grammar was typical for his age group. Now aged eleven, Jim shows no evidence of any problem with language, and his performance at school in reading and writing has been normal. He is even becoming proficient at sign language.

At the time that Jim entered the speech therapy programme, his younger brother Glenn was twenty months old and used no speech, although he too had normal hearing. Glenn's language acquisition is also instructive for any consideration of the importance of adult-child verbal interactions. Compared to other hearing children Glenn did not have much experience of conversation with adults, but by the time Glenn was two years old his elder brother's speech was approximately normal for his age. His interactions with his brother plus the adult speech addressed to him in roughly biweekly test and therapy sessions were sufficient for Glenn's language development to be essentially normal.

These observations suggest that at least some minimal exposure to verbal interactions with speakers of the language and perhaps some degree of simplification of the speech that the child hears are necessary for normal language acquisition, but they do not pin down what particular aspects of those experiences are the crucial ones. Several important features of verbal interactions between parent and child were absent from the television conversations heard by Jim. The objects and events referred to by the people on television are not typically present for the viewer to see; nonverbal indicators of the topic of conversation are greatly degraded; and the speech on all but the simplest of children's programmes is rapid and grammatically complex. Jim's viewing of television was rather indiscriminate, so he was not just exposed to *Sesame Street* or *Mr Rogers' Neighborhood* – one of the researchers tells of arriving at the house to see Jim watching a transvestite on a talk show expounding on the virtues of his lifestyle.

Other studies have tried to determine whether more specific aspects of the normal conversations between parent and child might facilitate language acquisition. Mothers frequently expand or rephrase their children's utterances. A child who says 'Doggy eat' may have his sentence expanded into 'Yes, the doggy is eating his bone'; if he says 'Dolly fall' he may hear 'Oh dear, the dolly fell over'. In this way the mother fills in the grammatical features that the child left out and also supplies more information about the situation that the child's utterance described. There are substantial individual differences in the frequency with which mothers indulge in such expansions. Some mothers expand very few utterances, others expand as many as 30 per cent of their children's sentences. Nevertheless, expansions might provide an important learning experience for the child. Immediately following his utterance the child hears the full grammatical form of that sentence without any change in its meaning.

How might we find out if expansions facilitate language acquisition? One thing we can do is to look at the relationship between the frequency of parental expansions and the rate of language acquisition of their children. If expansions do help, then children whose parents expand their sentences a great deal should be linguistically more advanced than children of the same age whose parents do not expand many sentences. In the earliest study of mothers' expansions, the child whose mother expanded her utterances the most was in fact the most precocious in her language development, but only three children were studied. Later studies that looked at more children did not find the same relationship, however; the frequency with which mothers expanded utterances did not predict their children's linguistic sophistication.

Another approach takes groups of children matched for age, intelligence, and level of language development. One group is exposed to systematic expansions of their sentences, another is not. Three studies of this sort have been carried out.[7] They differed in the duration of the period of intervention, in whether the children's mothers or trained tutors did the expanding, and in what proportion of the children's utterances were expanded. But none of the studies found any significant effect of the expansions on the children's language learning.

Why did expansions fail to enhance acquisition in these

experimental studies? One possibility is that expansions simply do not help the child, but there remain some weaknesses in the studies themselves. Occasional expansions serve to confirm the relationship between the child's utterance and the situation it describes. But the continued expansion of most or all of the child's sentences in these studies may have diluted the effectiveness of that confirmation, so the children may have stopped paying attention to the adults' sentences. In the most complete of the three studies, the largest language gains were actually made by a group of children whose sentences were not directly expanded but were followed instead by a further comment about the situation from the tutor. A child in this group who said 'Doggy eat' might hear 'Yes, the doggy is hungry'. This suggests that the richness and variety of the language input to the child may be more important than frequent expansions.

The importance of the richness of the parents' responses to what the child says has been confirmed in two studies by Keith Nelson.[8] In one study the researchers expanded the children's incomplete sentences, but they also *recast* complete utterances into a different grammatical form. A child who said 'Doggy eat' might have his sentence recast into a question about the same information: 'What is the doggy eating?' When the child made a comment about some aspect of the situation, the researcher kept that topic constant, but provided the child with a different way of talking about it. Children whose sentences were recast in this way later performed better on a sentence-imitation test than children who interacted with the researchers for the same period but whose utterances were not recast. The spontaneous speech of the recast-sentence group was also grammatically more complex than that of the children who did not hear recast sentences.

In the second study, Nelson demonstrated that the effects of recast sentences were selective. Children whose sentences were recast into complex questions showed improvement in the use of those question forms; children whose utterances were recast into sentences containing complex verbs later showed a greater use of those verbs in their own speech. The question group did not show much improvement in the use of verbs, and the verb group did not improve much in their use of complex questions.

Recastings of children's sentences are present but not very frequent in the speech of mothers, so they presumably do not play any large role in normal language development. Why do they enhance language acquisition when their frequency is increased? The recast sentences in Nelson's experimental studies possibly attracted the child's attention to the comparison between his own utterance and what the researcher then said about the same situation. The complex question and verb forms were present, though infrequent, in the speech of the mothers of these children, so the researchers were not introducing altogether new forms, just drawing attention to them. Taken together, these studies suggest that expansions and sentence recasts may not be very important in the normal verbal interaction between mother and child. But they also suggest that the best environment for learning language contains a rich variety of sentences closely tied to what the child currently produces. A moderate degree of novelty in the sentence forms the adult uses to talk about the situations that he shares with the child seems to draw the child's attention to those forms and so enhances his grammatical development.

It is commonly believed that parents correct their children's language errors, and that these corrections play an important role in language acquisition. This seems to be more true for some features of language than for others. Parents often correct their children when they use the wrong word for an object; if a child overextends a word to an inappropriate object his parents usually provide the correct word for that object. This is bound to help the child's word learning. Parents also frequently correct pronunciation errors, especially in older children. But for long periods of time children do not seem sensitive to those corrections. Little children will persist in producing systematic simplifications of the adult pronunciation of words even though their parents may try to correct them. As we mentioned earlier, our son Nicholas went from correctly pronouncing *turtle* at the age of fifteen months to pronouncing it as *kurka* at eighteen months. Systematic attempts to correct his pronunciation over a period of two months had no effect and the following interaction was typical:

Peter: Say *tur*.
Nicholas: *Tur*.
Peter: Say *till*.
Nicholas: *Till*.
Peter: Say *turtle*.
Nicholas: *Kurka*.

At twenty months Nicholas could produce the component syllables correctly but not the whole word regardless of how often we corrected him. Thus while corrections of pronunciation may have a long-term effect on the child, they do not usually have any immediate effect.

Parents do not often directly correct grammatical errors in little children, although their expansions of the child's incomplete sentences may function as indirect corrections. Furthermore, it has been argued that children are not sensitive to the rare grammatical corrections that adults do supply. Most of the evidence for this is anecdotal, and a frequently cited example is the following interaction between a child and her mother.[9]

Child: My teacher holded the rabbits and we patted them.

Mother: Did you say your teacher held the baby rabbits?

Child: Yes.

Mother: What did you say she did?

Child: She holded the baby rabbits and we patted them.

Mother: Did you say she held them tightly?

Child: No, she holded them loosely.

Nevertheless, children clearly do learn from the discrepancy between what they say and the way that adults produce the same sentence form. The point seems to be that there are only certain periods in the child's mastery of a grammatical form during which he is sensitive to such a discrepancy. The following conversation between Peter and a thirty-month-old child represents a case in which the child was suddenly aware of the discrepancy between her own rules and that of the adult to whom she was talking. At the beginning of the interaction Katie had a common overgeneralization in her speech: all possessive pronoun forms ended in *s*. So *its*, *his*, *hers*, *ours*, *theirs* and *yours* were appropriately produced, but mine became *mines*. The dialogue between Katie and Peter concerns a number of grimy pieces of Playdo whose ownership was being disputed:

Katie: Don't crush mines up!

Peter: What was yours? What was it? Had you made it into something?

Katie: Dis is mines.

Peter: That's yours, OK.

So far, this interchange supports Katie's notion that possessive pronouns end in *s*, but the argument continues:

Katie: Dat's yours.
Peter: That's mine. OK. I'll keep that. Is that as well?
I have lots of pieces now, don't I?
Katie: Dis is mine.
Peter: Hm-mm.

Katie has noticed that *mine* does not have an *s* on the end. But now she is uncertain about the rule:

Peter: Did you steal some more? You stole some more!
Keep stealing all mine, don't you?
Katie: I keep stealing all your.

The exception has now become the rule! Katie needed more exposure to the set of pronouns before she could work out that *mine* was the exception, but this play session seemed to have helped her notice the discrepancy between her *mines* and the adult *mine*.

Another common belief about the process of language learning is that parents reward their children for speaking properly so that grammatical sentences become more frequent and ill-formed sentences drop out. If this is the case, the rewards must be quite subtle. It is simply not the case that parents selectively reward grammatically correct sentences with verbal approval. Parents tend to see through incorrect grammar to the meaning the child is trying to express, and they approve or disapprove of that rather than the grammar. For example, one two-year-old said, 'Mama isn't boy, he a girl', and her mother replied, 'That's right', but when another child said, 'Walt Disney comes on Tuesday', his mother said firmly, 'No, he does not', although the child's sentence was perfectly grammatical.[10] Verbal encouragement or disapproval appears to be closely tied to the age and language sophistication of the child, and may be used only in extreme cases. Thus an eighteen-month-old who suddenly came out with a long sentence would receive enthusiastic praise from his parents; a five-year-old who began talking like a two-year-old would probably be corrected and admonished. A certain amount of verbal encouragement in the early stages of language development may help the child by providing both motivation to try to communicate and a confirmation of the success of that communication.

Surely, though, the child will be more likely to get his message across if he speaks grammatically, and correct sentences will be favoured in communication. Looking at the interactions between thirty-month-olds and their parents, however, one finds few, if any, misunderstandings between them. Although many grammatical features are still missing from their speech, the children supply enough to go with the context to make their meaning plain. Children's mastery of English tag questions at three or four years of age also indicates that pressure to communicate does not determine the learning of complex grammatical forms. Tag questions are the little requests for confirmation that English people in particular add to the end of their sentences. So one might say, 'It is a lovely day, isn't it?' or 'John loves cross-country skiing, doesn't he?' and expect one's listener to answer, 'Yes'. The formation of tag questions requires knowledge of much of the grammar of English – how to form negative questions, how to shorten them to just an auxiliary verb and a pronoun, and how to make the pronoun agree in number and person with the subject of the sentence. But there is an easier way to accomplish the same communicative effect, and children begin with that. They simply tag the expression *right* or *hey* on to the end of their sentences: 'It is a lovely day, right?' Still they go on to learn the full adult form, although they can communicate the tag question's request for confirmation just as effectively with the simpler form.

Once again the effects of communication success or failure on language learning seem to be related to age.

A child in the one- or two-word stage is far more likely to be misunderstood than an older child, so pressure to communicate more effectively may well contribute to the motivation for early learning. What the child finds rewarding may depend on his level of language development. When the child first begins to produce words, parental attention and encouragement, or obtaining the objects he desires, may constitute the motivation to learn new words. Later on, as he develops a simple grammar, being understood and communicating his desires more effectively may become important. Finally, sounding like an adult might be sufficient reward for learning.

Many behaviour modification programmes have used explicit rewards such as verbal approval, displays of affection, or sweets and other food to teach quite extensive verbal repertoires to severely retarded and autistic children.[11] The children are systematically rewarded for producing sounds and then words that approximate those spoken by the therapist. Finally, simple sentences and grammatical morphemes or short conversational sequences are taught to the child. Children who were previously mute or had little appropriate speech learned to name objects, events and relationships, to make their desires known by verbal means, and to ask questions. Most children even progressed so far as to use the words and grammatical features in novel combinations that were not explicitly taught.

On the other hand, the long-term carryover of these trained language skills from the therapy situation to the child's speech in his everyday environment has been distressingly small. The abnormal child's ordinary environment does not typically dispense rewards like praise and food for much of his speech, and he can often obtain what he wants by gestures or crying; thus all too frequently the disordered child's advances in language have rapidly dissipated when he was transferred back to his home or institutional environment. The child's language must come to be maintained by the natural rewards for speech – social communication, gaining and transmitting information, obtaining what one wants, and similar functions – but we do not yet know how to transfer control of his speech from explicit rewards to these naturally occurring implicit ones. Furthermore, some of the social rewards for speech may simply not be effective for certain disordered children. Autistic children withdraw from social contact, but much of language serves to maintain social interaction. Behaviour modification programmes demonstrate that even severely retarded and autistic children can learn language skills in strict training procedures using powerful primary rewards, but for those advances to be maintained the children must either learn what language is good for in the natural environment, or the systematic rewards for speaking must be continued by his parents or caregivers.

To summarize, parents' responses to the normal child's sentences in the form of expansions, recasts and corrections, as well as their comprehension or misunderstanding of his speech, may all play a role in encouraging language learning in the child. However, none of these factors seems to be an important determinant of the *pattern* of language acquisition, and each seems to be effective only in certain contexts and at certain times. The stage of physical and intellectual development of the child, and any systematic biases or strategies that he may adopt in learning the language, seem to be more powerful determinants of the course of language development. It is those constraints on the rate and sequence of acquisition that we will turn to next.

8/Constraints on Learning

The seventeenth-century philosopher John Locke characterized the initial state of the child's mind as a blank slate. The child began with no innate preconceptions about his world, and all knowledge came to be written on the slate of the mind by the chalk of experience. Since that time debate has raged over the relative contribution of inheritance and experience to our knowledge, be it knowledge of the physical world or of language. For much of this century the stress was on the necessary experiences for language learning, but in the past fifteen years there has been a growing awareness that the process of language acquisition is limited by factors other than the child's experience of speech. The slate has certain inherent properties that impose a pattern on the writing of experience and set boundaries on its effects at different points in the child's growth.

BIOLOGICAL CONSTRAINTS

In Chapter 2 we suggested that human infants are predisposed to distinguish speech from other environmental sounds, and are particularly sensitive to sound differences that are important in many languages. But what about the more general properties of language? No other species shares with man his highly complex, creative and symbolic form of communication: could it be that we are innately endowed with the specific ability to learn such a system? Arguments about the answer to this question have taken two major forms. One concerns the abstractness of certain grammatical rules and the impossibility of learning them from the type of language that the child hears.[1] The second has captured the imagination of the public to a much greater extent and concerns the possibility of teaching a human language to any other animal. If we are uniquely endowed with a faculty for language, no other species should be able to learn our language. The most promising candidate for such training is the chimpanzee, man's closest relative among the apes. Early attempts to teach chimpanzees to speak did not work, owing to limitations on the chimps' control of the vocal tract.[2] The breakthrough came in deciding to exploit the natural talent of the chimp to make gestures. Several studies have now looked at the acquisition of the manual sign language of the deaf by young chimpanzees in an environment approximating that of the human child.[3]

How close have the chimpanzees come to learning a human language? In many respects there are close parallels between their language acquisition and early child language. All the chimps so far studied have quite rapidly acquired a vocabulary of a couple of hundred different signs. The content of their vocabulary is highly similar to that of young children – concrete nouns for food and other important things in their world, verbs that label actions, and adjectives like *big* and *sweet*. Many of the signs are iconic, that is, they resemble the objects they refer to: the sign for *cat* involves a pantomime of its whiskers, the sign for *hat* is made on the head, and so on. Words in spoken language do not often have this quality, except for words like *toot-toot* or *moo* that are standard babytalk. Chimpanzees are apparently aided by the iconic quality of signs, but their learning is not restricted to iconic signs. Other signs are quite arbitrary in form, and the chimps learn them too. Furthermore, the chimps' creative extension of signs to referents other than those for which they were first learned looks much like children's early use of words. Washoe, the first chimpanzee to acquire sign language, initially learned the sign *open* in connection with doors, but she then used it for opening boxes or a briefcase, and even for turning on a tap.

> Washoe learned the sign for *listen* for an alarm clock which signals meal time. She used the sign for other bells, for the sounds of people walking outside her trailer door, and for watches and clocks. She signed *listen* spontaneously when she found a broken watchband, and then when she saw a flashlight that blinks on and off. Washoe has a sign for *hurt* which she learned first with scratches or bruises. Later she used the same sign also for red stains, for a decal on the back of a person's hand, and the first time she saw a person's navel. (Klima and Bellugi, 1973, p. 99)

Washoe even created new signs for objects: the first time she saw a duck she spontaneously produced the combined sign *water-bird*.

The chimpanzees have not stopped with single signs, however. After a few months of learning signs, each of the chimps has spontaneously combined signs in ways that made sense to their human observers. For example, Washoe produced the following:

> open drink (for the water tap)
> key open please blanket (at the bedding cupboard)
> listen dog (at the sound of barking)

more tickle (for her companion to resume tickling Washoe)

Roger Washoe tickle (for Roger to tickle Washoe)

Washoe's observers noticed that she brought her hands down into a resting position only after the entire sequence of signs rather than after each sign, suggesting that she intended it to be treated as a unit. This is the equivalent in sign language to the use of intonation to signal the end of spoken utterances. If the chimpanzees' sign sequences are analysed as to the relational meanings they express, similarities to early child language are again apparent. Like children, the chimps talk about agents, actions and objects, possessor and possessed, attributes and objects, and locations.

On the other hand, it is not clear that they use the order of the signs to mark contrasts in meaning to the same extent that children use word order in speech. A recent report of the sign language of a chimpanzee, Nim, indicated that the chimp did show stable preferences in the ordering of particular signs but did not reliably use order to express the major relational meanings – agents were as likely to appear after actions as before them, the possessed object was often mentioned before the possessor, and so on.[4] A systematic analysis of the sign orders of the humans who converse with the chimpanzees is still not available, however, so it remains uncertain whether the chimps simply mirror the input to them. Sign language makes much less use of temporal order than spoken English does. Nevertheless, a recent study of young deaf children learning sign language documents their reliable use of sign order to convey the meaning of early sentences. Is it the case, then, that chimpanzees can combine signs to describe different aspects of a situation, but they cannot use grammatical rules like sign order to clarify their meanings? Such a conclusion does not seem warranted since the chimpanzee Washoe reportedly used sign order appropriately both to contrast meanings in her own signed sequences and to understand such contrasts as *boy kissed girl* versus *girl kissed boy*. It may be that young chimpanzees are just not as predisposed to use consistent ordering as young children, and it is likely that in the here-and-now contexts of their conversations with humans there is little pressure on them to be more precise: their meaning is clear from the situation. However, they can be trained to use order to carry meaning.

Other studies of the chimpanzee's capacity to learn language have employed systems of symbols.[5] The chimpanzee had to associate each symbol with its referent or functional meaning, and then learn to arrange them in sequence to convey a message. For example, one study used magnetic-backed pieces of plastic of various colours and shapes, which the chimp placed on a metal board. Sarah, the chimpanzee in this study, learned the names for food, actions, and people by putting the appropriate pieces of plastic on to the board in exchange for food rewards. The training and testing took place in a laboratory for a small amount of time each day, and Sarah was not given the use of the tokens any time she wished to communicate. Unlike the studies of the signing chimps, the goal of this project was not to see whether chimpanzees could pick up some language in natural circumstances, but rather to test the limits of the chimpanzee's logical and grammatical abilities under controlled conditions. The outcome of the project is a little disconcerting for those who view these abilities as the private reserve of mankind. The chimp Sarah learned a good-sized vocabulary of words that bear no iconic resemblance to their referents; they include such modifiers as *big* and *little*, *few* and *many*, *red* and *blue*, *round* and *square*, and such relations as *colour of*, *size of*, *shape of* and *name of*. The mastery of the last item means that she can now be taught a new word without extensive association between it and its referent. She is simply told, for instance:

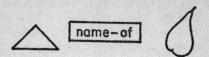

and then uses △ to label pears or to ask for them. She describes the properties of pears if she is shown △ and asked about its properties; in short, she does almost everything that we do with words.

In terms of grammar, Sarah was able to use the order of tokens as a guide to meaning in both comprehension and production. Furthermore, she seemed to be sensitive to the organization of the elements in a sentence. For instance, having been taught to understand such sentences as

Sarah banana pail insert. (Sarah put the banana in the pail.)

She was then taught compound sentences:

Sarah banana pail insert Sarah cracker dish insert.

Finally, she was tested with the redundant words deleted:

Sarah banana pail cracker dish insert.

To succeed at this task the chimp would have to recognize that *Sarah* applied to the whole sentence rather than to just the first few words; also with the word *insert*. Each food word would also have to be grouped with its respective container. The sentence has to be understood as a structured whole, for no simpler strategies would enable Sarah to succeed. On a series of such tests Sarah performed over 80 per cent correctly, considerably above chance.

The chimpanzees in these controlled studies have also proved capable of using new words in sentence contexts that they have never encountered in training. So Sarah, for instance, produced

Mary give pear Sarah.

without further training once she had learned to make sequences like

Mary give apple Sarah.

This is a minimal form of creativity but a very necessary one to show that the language of the chimp is governed by productive rules rather than learned by rote. Another sign of the creativity of Sarah's language use comes from an occasion on which she invented a conjunction of terms instead of producing two sentences as she had been trained. Confronted with a tempting piece of chocolate and an apple, instead of writing

Mary give apple Sarah.
Mary give chocolate Sarah.

she wrote,

Mary give apple chocolate Sarah.

Nevertheless, there is quite a difference between the admittedly remarkable accomplishments of the chimps and the final complexity of human languages. Our adult grammar has certain universal characteristics that render it distinct from any of the achievements of these chimpanzees. An example is its power to create highly complex sentences with relative clauses such as

This is the dog that chased the cat that ate the rat that lived in the house that Jack built.

Most native speakers of English can easily understand that sentence and others like it. Small children do not, and neither do young chimpanzees, but small children grow into adults who can understand them; chimpanzees seem not to do so. The more complex forms of grammar may therefore be beyond the grasp of the chimpanzee, and it is here that our unique language ability may lie. But it seems now incontrovertible that the chimpanzee is capable of acquiring a language much like that of the two- to three-year-old human child, at least the rudiments of human language.

Why might this be true of chimpanzees but not other animals? It seems that chimps share sufficient intelligence with us to enable them to learn a certain amount of language. What are the crucial features of this intelligence? One appears to be a capacity for representing objects and events by symbols that can then evoke the properties of the referents themselves. The word *apple*, or its corresponding plastic symbol or sign, conjures up as rich a concept as would the apple itself. Given the word, we can list the properties of apples as if we had one in front of us; so can the chimpanzee.

A necessary component of this capacity is the ability to hold objects in memory and the belief that they still exist when no longer in view. Very young children are unable to do this, but by twelve months of age or so, they have knowledge of the permanence of objects and vigorously search for an object when it is covered up. The great apes share that fundamental ability with us. In addition, chimpanzees apparently agree with us about the analysis of events: they recognize a difference between the agent and the thing affected, they understand simple cause-and-effect relations, and they share with us a visual system that is sensitive to colours, shapes, and sizes. Of course it is possible to conceive of a species with quite a different view of the world which might learn a language that emphasizes things we ignore and vice versa. But evolution does not seem to have provided us with an equally intelligent but different creature with which to compare the chimpanzee, unless the dolphin or porpoise proves to be a candidate. Attempts are now underway to teach porpoises a symbol language much like Sarah's.

PHYSICAL MATURITY

Profoundly deaf infants begin to babble at about the same age as hearing children, even though they cannot hear the speech of adults or their own vocalizations. Furthermore, common simplifications appear in the pronunciation of early words by normal children, regardless of what language they are learning: for example, multisyllable words tend to be pronounced as reduplicated syllables (*mama, dada*); consonants produced at the front of the mouth predominate over those produced at the back of the mouth; and clusters of consonants are reduced to single consonants. These findings suggest that early vocal development is significantly affected by the child's maturing control over his speech organs. This is not to say that the child's language environment is unimportant – deaf children stop babbling early and later experience great difficulty in learning to talk intelligibly unless hearing aids correct their hearing loss. It merely indicates that the physical maturity of the child constrains the rate and pattern of early speech development.

An even more important relationship may exist, however,

between physical maturation and language acquisition. Some researchers have postulated a *critical period* during which it is maximally easy to learn language. During the years from late infancy to puberty, language learning proceeds quickly, effortlessly, and without formal instruction. Put a young child down in a new language environment and he soon picks up the language around him and comes to speak it like a native of the community. After puberty, however, language learning seems to proceed more laboriously and is never as complete. Place an adult in a new language environment and, even with the help of formal teaching, he continues to sound like a foreigner. The critical-period hypothesis argues that physical changes at puberty somehow make the brain less adaptable so that language learning becomes more difficult.[6]

The notion of a critical period for learning is a familiar one in zoology. For example, male chaffinches acquire an intricate song that they use to attract a mate and declare their territorial and conjugal claims. But for a young male chaffinch to learn the full song, it must hear an adult singing the song and also hear its own attempts to reproduce that song during a critical time period. This period ends when the bird becomes sexually mature in the second spring of its life. If a young chaffinch is isolated from other chaffinches or temporarily deafened for this crucial period of time, no amount of later exposure to the normal song will correct the aberrant song it develops.[7]

What kind of evidence supports the existence of a similar critical period for language learning in humans? One longitudinal study found that the language development of severely retarded children stopped at puberty.[8] Though younger retarded children continued to learn from the speech addressed to them, retarded adolescents did not seem to pick up any more language from only hearing it spoken. After puberty, strict training procedures using extrinsic rewards for learning seem to be necessary to teach new language skills to the severely retarded. Other evidence comes from people whose language has been disrupted by damage to the areas of the brain that control speech. If the injury occurs in childhood, recovery of language is rapid and fairly complete, but after puberty, such damage results in much more permanent language loss.

A third possible source of evidence is the learning of a second language. There is no good evidence that learning the vocabulary and grammar of a new language becomes harder or follows a different pattern after puberty, provided the adult experiences the same extensive exposure to the language that the child gets. Adults make the same kinds of errors of omission and overgeneralization as children do in learning a new language: they may even learn it quicker than a five- or six-year-old because they know more about their own language and are generally more skilful learners. On the other hand, there is substantial evidence that one's accent becomes relatively immutable after puberty.[9] An adult learning a new language or dialect tends to retain his old accent so that he never sounds exactly like a native speaker. A child, however, is more likely to acquire a second language without any foreign accent. We all know immigrants who have retained a strong hint of their origins despite many years in our country. Similarly with regional accents: a Brooklyner in Chicago and a Cockney in Newcastle reveal their roots as soon as they speak, even though those roots may go back a long way. Their children, on the other hand, soon absorb the local dialect and cannot be distinguished from their peers. Second-language learning therefore suggests that the critical period applies more to the sounds of speech than to grammar or vocabulary.

In order to establish the existence and duration of a critical period for learning, biologists perform a controlled deprivation experiment. The animal is deprived for varying periods of time of those experiences thought to be necessary for learning: if the time of deprivation covers the critical period, no learning will result from subsequent exposure to those experiences. Clearly such an experiment, in which children hear no oral language or see no sign language until after the postulated end of the critical period, cannot be carried out for ethical reasons. Over the centuries, however, there have been scattered reports of children whose upbringing has approximated just such a degree of isolation from language. Perhaps the most celebrated case is that of the wild boy of Aveyron, a child found running wild in the woods of southern France in 1800.[10] He was taken in by a dedicated educationalist Dr Jean-Marc-Gaspard Itard, who named him Victor and tried to teach him language and other social skills. Itard's efforts are described in his book about Victor, *De l'éducation d'un homme sauvage,* and dramatized in a wonderful film by François Truffaut called *L'Enfant sauvage.* Victor was thought to be about eleven or twelve when found, and as far as could be determined his hearing was normal. But despite Itard's attempts to train him, Victor never learned to say more than a word or two. Unfortunately, so little is known about Victor's childhood that we cannot rule out the possibility that he was brain-damaged or retarded. Thus his failure to learn language does not confirm the existence of a critical period for language acquisition.

In November of 1970 a startling case came to the attention of the Los Angeles authorities. A child was discovered in the upstairs room of a suburban house, a child whose isolation and neglect rival that of any earlier wild child. When found, Genie was thirteen years and seven months old, past puberty, but weighing only sixty pounds. She could not chew any solid food, was incontinent, and unable to stand erect. Questioning of her parents revealed that from the age of twenty months, Genie had been confined to a small curtained room, strapped down in an infant cot or tied to a potty chair. If she made any noises she was likely to be beaten by her father, who did not speak to her but would occasionally bark at her like a dog. She was visited for only a few minutes each day by her mother, during which time she was fed with baby food but few, if any, words were addressed to her. There was no television or radio in the house since the father could not tolerate noise, so Genie did not hear any language from those sources either. The available paediatric records, though scanty, reveal that her first twenty months were unremarkable, but the fact that she was delayed in walking because of a congenital hip dislocation had led her father to conclude that she was hopelessly retarded.

When Genie was discovered, she was severely disturbed emotionally, having frequent silent tantrums, but there were no other clear symptoms of autism. She had normal hearing, vision, and eye-hand co-ordination, and the fact that she had learned to use a few single words before the age of twenty months suggests that she was not mentally retarded. When tested soon after her rescue, however, she was mute, could understand only a few words and simple commands, and revealed no comprehension of grammar. Genie therefore supplies the strongest test of all the wild children for or against the existence of a critical period for language acquisition.[11]

For the past seven years Genie has lived in a foster home and has acquired English primarily from exposure to speech rather than explicit training, much as a normal child would. In many respects Genie's progressive mastery of a first language has mirrored that of normal children. Like those normal children, her earliest words consisted of consonant-vowel monosyllables and longer words only entered her speech later. She simplified initial consonant clusters like *sp-*, *st-* and *sk-* by deleting the /s/, and either deleted or simplified final consonant clusters. Although over- and underextensions of her early words have not been reported, she generalized the words that she learned for specific objects to other objects of the same sort. *Dog* was first learned with respect to a specific pet, but was immediately used for other dogs. Her earliest two-word utterances expressed the relations attribute-entity and possessor-possessed, and soon afterwards agent-action and action-object forms appeared. As in normal development, these two-word phrases then became elements in longer sentences, such as agent-action-object sentences. Finally, she first produced negative sentences by appending *no* to the beginning of the utterance, just as a normal child does.

Nevertheless, differences from the normal course of acquisition have also appeared. Genie's rules of sound combination and substitution, though similar to those of normal children, seem to be more variably applied than they are by normal children, and after seven years of language acquisition she continues to have articulation problems. Several aspects of her mastery of word and sentence meanings suggest that her intellectual development was more in advance of her language development than it usually is in first-language acquisition. For example, colour words and numbers appeared much earlier in her vocabulary than they do for normal children. She also seemed to understand all *wh*-questions at about the same time. Young children usually master *what* and *where* much earlier than *why*, *when* and *how*, presumably because the latter are conceptually more difficult.

Finally, Genie has still not acquired certain important features of English that are generally learned before the age of four. Her use of word order shows peculiar inconsistencies: although her own speech is unfailingly correct in ordering the elements of the sentences, she does not use word-order information in comprehending simple noun-verb-noun sequences like *The boy pulled the girl*. Her speech lacks most auxiliary verbs, and she still does not produce deictic expressions like personal pronouns and the demonstrative adjectives *this* and *that*. Although she comprehends most question forms and has been specifically trained to ask some questions, Genie does not spontaneously ask new questions as normal children do in such great profusion around the age of three or four.

Considering her upbringing, Genie has made giant strides in both her social behaviour and her language, but she remains limited in her use of language and in her control of more complex language forms. She still reveals some emotional and social difficulties, but is able to function quite well in her foster home and in special classes at school. But what can we say about the critical-period hypothesis in the light of Genie's language learning? First, any strong version that holds that a child must acquire a first language before puberty or he will be unable to learn from subsequent exposure to speech must be wrong. Genie had minimal experience of speech prior to puberty; yet she has acquired a substantial amount of language without formal instruction. On the other hand, a weaker version of the critical-period hypothesis, stating that first-language learning is more difficult and incomplete after puberty, may still be true. In almost seven years Genie has made about as much progress in language acquisition as a young normal child makes in two or three years. Genie's continuing difficulty with articulation also agrees with the evidence from second-language learning that there may be a critical period for the acquisition of patterns of pronunciation.

Nevertheless, the case of Genie does not conclusively support even the weaker critical-period hypothesis. The circumstances of Genie's early life hardly approximate the perfect deprivation experiment in biology. Genie was not only deprived of the opportunity to hear speech or to converse with others; she also suffered severe malnutrition, chronic social deprivation, and other maltreatment. The extent to which her language difficulties reflect the effects of these additional deprivations rather than just her isolation from speech during childhood cannot be determined. We cannot completely rule out the existence of brain dysfunction resulting from these other factors.

In short, physical maturation does seem to constrain the rate and pattern of vocal development, and there may well be a critical period for the establishment of patterns of articulation, but the evidence in favour of a more general critical period for language acquisition remains inconclusive.

LINGUISTIC CONSTRAINTS

The nature of the language that the child is learning also constrains the sequence of acquisition. The fewer or simpler the grammatical rules involved in a construction, the easier it is to learn; so simpler constructions precede more complex constructions in acquisition, provided that frequency of exposure is kept fairly constant. Consider the case of two children who concurrently acquired Hungarian and Serbo-Croatian, with roughly equal amounts of exposure to each language.[12] In Hungarian the locative expressions corresponding to *into, out of, on to,* and so on, are marked by inflections on the noun. There is no grammatical gender in the language, so regardless of what noun an inflection is applied to, it remains the same. By contrast, the same locative expressions in Serbo-Croatian are grammatically complex. In addition to an inflection on the noun, a locative preposition is required. The noun differs in case (genitive, dative, and so on) depending on the preposition that is used; the form of the inflection varies with the gender and final sound of the noun as well as with the preposition. The two bilingual children expressed locative relationships in Hungarian and Serbo-Croatian at about the same time, saying things like *Doll drawer* while putting a doll into a drawer. But they used the full grammatical form for the locative in Hungarian some months before they could master either the inflections or the prepositions in Serbo-Croatian.

One can also look at the relative complexity of sentence forms within a single language. Children learning English produce simple active sentences:

He can drive.

before they can turn them into negatives,

He can't drive.

or questions,

Can he drive?

or can truncate them,

He can.

Still later to appear are sentences that involve a combination of two of these forms, such as negative questions,

Can't he drive?

or truncated questions,

Can he?

or truncated negatives,

He can't.

Tag questions like:

He can drive, can't he?

require all of the grammatical knowledge that goes into making questions, negatives, and truncated sentences, and they do not usually appear in children's speech until all of the simpler forms have occurred. In brief, the complexity of the grammatical knowledge required to use a construction accurately predicts the sequence of acquisition of many sentence forms.[13]

INTELLECTUAL CONSTRAINTS

In discussing the chimpanzee's ability to learn a human language we mentioned a few intellectual achievements that may be prerequisites for learning to use words to refer to objects. The child, and the chimpanzee, must recognize the identity of an object across certain changes in its appearance: it is the same object despite changes in position, orientation, distance or movement. This is a very early realization and may even be innate in the human infant; without it, it is unlikely that the child could associate a word with an object. More sophisticated, and later to develop, is the notion of object permanence. Without the awareness that objects continue to exist even when they are out of sight, it is unlikely that a child could talk about an object in its absence.

Intellectual maturity limits later language development as well. For example, hypothetical statements such as

If it is windy we shall fly the kite.
If it had snowed we should have lost our way.

do not usually appear in children's speech until they are four or five years old. They are conceptually difficult, requiring an ability to conceive of possibilities rather than actualities, and an ability to shift one's reference point in time to the past or future. Children acquiring English seem to learn all of the component linguistic forms that go into making a hypothetical statement some time before they actually produce hypotheticals.[14] More remarkably, the grammatical complexity of the hypothetical form in a language does not seem to be an important determinant of the age at which it is mastered. In Russian the hypothetical is grammatically simple, but children do not use it until around the same age as English-speaking children.[15] The emergence of the hypothetical statement in children's speech therefore seems to await understanding of the concept of the hypothetical, rather than the grammar.

SYSTEMATIC BIASES OR STRATEGIES

A number of regularities in the pattern of language development seem to arise from inherent biases that children bring to the task of learning language. For example, the ends of words appear to be more salient to the child than the beginnings of words. Provided that the forms are equated for conceptual difficulty and frequency in the language, suffixes and postpositions are acquired before prefixes and prepositions. In some cases the ends of the words are stressed, so that portion stands out. Young children typically omit unstressed syllables from words: they say *raffe* for *giraffe*, *narna* for *banana*, *mato* for *tomato*. However, even in languages like Czech, where the initial syllables of all words are stressed, the ends of words appear to be more salient for the child, and initial syllables and prepositions are often omitted. The article in Bulgarian is a noun suffix and is acquired by children much earlier than articles in English or German, which precede the noun.

Another common bias that children bring to language learning is the avoidance of exceptions. A classic example of this is the development of the English past tense. Irregular past tenses like *broke* for *break* are typically replaced for a time by an overgeneralization of the regular *-ed* ending, *breaked*. As a corollary of this, general rules are typically learned before rules for special cases. Russian children typically begin by using a single inflection for the accusative form of all nouns; only later do they learn that masculine animate nouns in Russian take a special accusative inflection.

Sometimes children appear to adopt quite systematic strategies for interpreting unfamiliar forms. Many children go through a stage of interpreting any noun-verb-noun sequence as expressing the relationship agent-actor-object. This is, of course, appropriate for the simple active sentences that the child frequently hears, but just the opposite interpretation is correct for the much rarer passive sentence: the object is first, the agent is last. For a time, then, these children systematically misunderstand reversible passive sentences like *The truck was bumped by the car*, when their meaning is not apparent from the context.[16]

The strategies used in acquiring language are sometimes very general across different languages. At an early stage in the acquisition of words for temporal relations in English, French or German, children rely on the order of mention of the events as a cue to their relationship in time. In their own speech they describe events in the order in which they happened, and in comprehension they interpret the first thing mentioned as having happened first.[17] They therefore have no problems with such sentences as:

The farmer watered the garden before he planted the corn.

After he watered the garden, the farmer planted the corn.

But they make errors on:

Before the boy ate the peach, he washed his hands.
The boy ate the peach after he washed his hands.

In many cases, however, there are substantial individual differences in the strategies adopted. For example, some children imitate any parental utterance that contains a new word but expresses a relational meaning familiar to the child. Imitation is for them a way of acquiring new words. Other children selectively imitate parental utterances that contain words the children know but express meanings that they have not yet mastered in their own speech. Imitation is for them a way of expressing new sentence meanings. Some children imitate a great many of their parents' words and sentences, others imitate almost none.[18]

We still understand very little about where such biases or strategies come from. Some may be common to the child's learning of many different skills, others may be restricted to his acquisition of language. Some may derive from the parents' speech to the child, or from the ways in which they react to his uses of language; for example, some parents may encourage imitation, others may not. Other biases may be an outgrowth of the child's stage of intellectual development at the time, and may relate to the limitations in his memory or to the characteristic ways in which he organizes his knowledge.

Researchers who study early language have become increasingly conscious of individual differences in language acquisition. There may well be several alternative routes to the mastery of the full adult language. Some children learn a large number of words before they begin to combine them into sentences, others produce multiword utterances as soon as they have a working vocabulary of fifty words or so. A few children begin by learning words for things and actions, others first learn words that express their desires or direct other people's behaviour.[19] The documentation of these individual differences and the range of normal variation in the rate and pattern of language development is crucial for determining the nature and extent of many language disorders. But it is also important to our understanding of the process of first-language learning that we continue to seek the sources of these individual differences, be they in the child's intellectual or physical development, in his interaction with his parents, or in the particular language input that he gets.

9/Conclusion

From time to time in this book we have indicated actions that parents can take to help their child over a particular hurdle and on to a better understanding of language and the rules by which the game is played. In Chapter 4, for example, we underlined the usefulness to the child of hearing a large number of conversations that include *why* questions and answers so that he can develop a sense of when it is appropriate to ask *why* and what constitutes an acceptable answer to that kind of question. In Chapter 7 we talked about the way in which parents seem to tailor their usually complex, and even ungrammatical, language so that they are speaking in short, simple and correct sentences to their young children, as if deliberately offering the best language model they can.

Parents do model language behaviour, just as they model other kinds of behaviour. Young children imitate sounds, including regional pronunciations; inflections such as the questioning 'isn't it?' which the British seem to use at the end of every other sentence or the similar, rhetorical 'eeeeh?' used to end conversational remarks in parts of Africa. Of course, parents are not the only influence. Brothers, sisters and other close relatives or friends contribute, and sometimes it is possible to hear the familiar phrases of one person woven into the vocal compositions of a child. Even more remote people can have an effect, and a child's attention may be caught by phrases heard during a chance encounter. Especially as they begin school, children may deliberately use words or expressions picked up from new friends in order to try out their newly felt roles as members of a larger society. In voicing a degree of independence and taking steps of this kind, they begin to play with language as a mode of communication – not only by using words to state a particular idea but by counting on the manner of stating it to say something about where they are in the journey from within the family to out in the world. Nevertheless, to parents, the role of language model may seem like an awesome responsibility. There is the danger that, having obtained more information about language acquisition, they may feel they should move past a superficial watchfulness about the language they use to a more self-conscious presentation of it.

That was never the intent of this book. If there is anything that would seem more open to ridicule than the picture of scholars earnestly listening to the babble of infants, it would be the prospect of scholars teaching parents how to teach children to talk – the fact is that parents don't need it and children don't need it either. Language acquisition is one of the most robust processes at work during childhood. In normal circumstances, children learn to speak, and they often learn even in special circumstances. We have cited cases of children whose environment or development, or both working together, presented special obstacles of one kind or another in order to show the insights that can be gained by comparing cases of normal and special development. But the examples also testify to the extraordinary resiliency and vigour of the urge to communicate.

This is not to say that all children learn language equally soon, make exactly comparable strides, or ultimately become articulate in the same ways. With age, use of language becomes increasingly complex, judged not only by the sophistication of words or intricacy of syntax but also by the sense of character it conveys about any individual. This variety is apparent in the early primary grades among classmates writing stories: some stories are bold in tone, some are cautious; some pupils are developing a sense of humour, others are revealing an eye for detail, still others a flair for metaphor. As they grow, all children, including children in the same family, will develop distinctive points of view and modes of speaking. Over time each will influence the other: language starts out as a reflection of what the child knows; it becomes an influence that shapes how he thinks. Developed human language – in spite of what is known so far about the chimpanzees – offers us unique capabilities. With it, we can ask an infinite number of questions and expect some answers, convey descriptions, ponder possibilities in the mind without actually acting on them, and relay past experiences to those who did not witness it first hand. It is exciting to watch a child learn language, exciting for psychologists curious about the human mind, but most of all, perhaps, for parents interested in the unique individual who is emerging before their eyes.

References

1 THREE QUESTIONS

1. A. Gregoire, *L'Apprentissage du langage*, 2 vols. (Paris: Librairie Droz, 1937, 1949). W. F. Leopold, *Speech Development of a Bilingual Child*, 4 vols. (Evanston: Northwestern University Press, 1939–49). A. F. Chamberlain and J. C. Chamberlain, 'Studies of a Child', *Pedagogical Seminary*, 1904, *11*, 264–91. H. V. Velten, 'The Growth of Phonemic and Lexical Patterns in Infant Language', *Language*, 1943, *19*, 281–92.
2. D. I. Slobin and C. A. Welsh, 'Elicited Imitation as a Research Tool in Developmental Psycholinguistics'. In C. A. Ferguson and D. I. Slobin, eds., *Studies of Child Language Development* (New York: Holt, Rinehart and Winston, 1973).
3. L. M. Bloom, 'Talking, Understanding and Thinking'. In R. L. Schiefelbusch and L. L. Lloyd, eds., *Language Perspectives: Acquisition, Retardation and Intervention* (Baltimore: University Park Press, 1974).
4. J. Berko, 'The Child's Learning of English Morphology', *Word*, 1958, *14*, 150–77.

2 SOUNDS

1. E. C. Butterfield and G. N. Siperstein, 'Influence of Contingent Auditory Stimulation Upon Non-nutri-

tional Suckle'. In *Proceedings of the Third Symposium on Oral Sensation and Perception: The Mouth of the Infant* (Springfield, Ill.: Charles C. Thomas, 1974).

2. D. L. Molfese, 'Cerebral Asymmetry in Infants, Children and Adults: Auditory Evoked Responses to Speech and Musical Stimuli', *Journal of the Acoustical Society of America*, 1973, *53*, 363.

3. P. D. Eimas, 'Linguistic Processing of Speech by Young Infants'. In R. L. Schiefelbusch and L. L. Lloyd, eds., *Language Perspectives: Acquisition, Retardation and Intervention* (Baltimore: University Park Press, 1974). E. C. Butterfield and G. F. Cairns, 'Discussion Summary: Infant Reception Research'. In R. L. Schiefelbusch and L. L. Lloyd, eds., *Language Perspectives: Acquisition, Retardation and Intervention* (Baltimore: University Park Press, 1974).

4. P. Tallal and M. Piercy, 'Developmental Aphasia: Rate of Auditory Processing and Selective Impairment of Consonant Perception', *Neuropsychologia*, 1974, *12*, 83–93.

5. O. K. Garnica, 'The Development of Phonemic Speech Perception'. In T. E. Moore, ed., *Cognitive Development and the Acquisition of Language* (New York and London: Academic Press, 1973).

6. E. L. Kaplan, 'The Role of Intonation in the Acquisition of Language' (diss., Cornell University, 1969).

7. D. L. Olmsted, *Out of the Mouth of Babes* (The Hague: Mouton, 1971).

8. P. Lieberman, *Intonation, Perception and Language* (Cambridge, Mass.: MIT Press, 1967).

9. H. L. Rheingold, J. L. Gerwitz and H. W. Ross, 'Social Conditioning of Vocalizations in the Infant', *Journal of Comparative and Physiological Psychology*, 1959, *52*, 68–73. G. Todd and B. Palmer, 'Social Reinforcement of Infant Babbling', *Child Development*, 1968, *39*, 591–6.

10. S. Nakazima, 'A Comparative Study of the Speech Developments of Japanese and American English in Childhood', *Studies in Phonology*, 1962, *2*, 27–39.

11. B. J. Dodd, 'Effects of Social and Vocal Stimulation on

Infant Babbling', *Developmental Psychology*, 1972, 7, 80–3.

12. W. Leopold, *Speech Development of a Bilingual Child: A Linguist's Record, Volume 2: Sound Learning in the First Two Years* (Evanston, Ill.: Northwestern University Press, 1947).

13. D. Ingram, 'Current Issues in Child Phonology'. In D. M. Morehead and A. E. Morehead, eds., *Normal and Deficient Language* (Baltimore: University Park Press, 1976).

14. D. K. Oller, L. A. Wieman, W. J. Doyle and C. Ross, 'Infant Babbling and Speech', *Journal of Child Language*, 1976, 3, 1–12.

15. N. V. Smith, *The Acquisition of Phonology: A Case Study* (Cambridge: Cambridge University Press, 1973).

3 WORDS

1. E. V. Clark, 'What's in a Word? On the Child's Acquisition of Semantics in his First Language'. In T. E. Moore, ed., *Cognitive Development and the Acquisition of Language* (New York and London: Academic Press, 1973).

2. M. F. Bowerman, 'The Acquisition of Word Meaning: An Investigation of Some Current Conflicts'. In N. Waterson and C. Snow, eds., *Proceedings of the Third International Child Language Symposium* (New York: Wiley, 1977).

3. J. M. Anglin, *Word, Object, and Conceptual Development* (New York: Norton, 1977).

4. R. W. Brown, *Words and Things* (New York: Free Press, 1958).

5. K. Nelson, 'Structure and Strategy in Learning to Talk', *Monographs of the Society for Research in Child Development*, 1973, 38, No. 149.

6. W. Miller and S. Ervin, 'The Development of Grammar in Child Language'. In U. Bellugi and R. W. Brown, eds., *The Acquisition of Language. Monographs of the Society for Research in Child Development*, 1964,

29, No. 92, 9–34. L. M. Bloom, *One Word at a Time: The Use of Single Word Utterances Before Syntax* (The Hague: Mouton, 1973).

7. J. S. Bruner, 'From Communication to Language: A Psychological Perspective', *Cognition*, 1975, *3*, 255–87.

4 RULES

1. R. W. Brown, *A First Language: The Early Stages* (Cambridge: Harvard University Press, 1973; London: Allen & Unwin, 1973).

2. J. Dooley, 'Language Acquisition and Down's Syndrome: A Study of Early Semantics and Syntax (diss., Harvard University, 1976).

3. E. Tanouye, K. Lifter and L. Bloom, 'Verb Semantics and Grammatical Morphemes'. Paper presented to the Biennial Conference of the Society for Research in Child Development, New Orleans, 1977.

4. N. Katz, E. Baker and J. Macnamara, 'What's in a Name? A Study of How Children Learn Common and Proper Names', *Child Development*, 1974, *65*, 469–73.

5. R. W. Brown, 'Linguistic Determinism and Part of Speech', *Journal of Abnormal and Social Psychology*, 1957, *55*, 1–5.

6. U. Bellugi, 'The Acquisition of Negation' (diss., Harvard University, 1967).

7. E. S. Klima and U. Bellugi, 'Syntactic Regularities in the Speech of Children'. In J. Lyons and R. J. Wales, eds., *Psycholinguistics Papers* (Edinburgh: Edinburgh University Press, 1966).

8. R. W. Brown, 'The Development of Wh-Questions in Child Speech', *Journal of Verbal Learning and Verbal Behavior*, 1968, *7*, 279–90.

9. K. Hakuta, 'Learning to Speak a Second Language: What Exactly Does the Child Learn?' In D. P. Dato, ed., *Georgetown University Round Table on Languages and Linguistics* (Washington: Georgetown University Press, 1975).

10. M. Blank, 'Mastering the Intangible Through Language'. In D. Aaronson and R. W. Rieber, eds., *Developmental Psycholinguistics and Communication Disorders. Annals of the New York Academy of Sciences*, 1975, *263*, 44–58.

5 RELATIONSHIPS

1. S. Carey, 'The Child as Word Learner'. In M. Halle, J. Bresnan and G. A. Miller, eds., *Linguistic Theory and Psychological Reality* (Cambridge: MIT Press, 1978).
2. E. V. Clark, 'On the Child's Acquisition of Antonyms in Two Semantic Fields', *Journal of Verbal Learning and Verbal Behavior*, 1972, *11*, 750–8.
3. H. H. Clark and E. V. Clark, *Psychology and Language: An Introduction to Psycholinguistics* (New York: Harcourt Brace Jovanovich, 1977).
4. P. A. de Villiers and J. G. de Villiers, 'On This, That, and the Other: Nonegocentrism in Very Young Children', *Journal of Experimental Child Psychology*, 1974, *18*, 438–47.
5. E. V. Clark, 'From Gesture to Word: On the Natural History of Deixis in Language Acquisition'. In J. Bruner and A. Garton, eds., *Human Growth and Development*, Wolfson College Lectures, 1976 (Oxford: Oxford University Press, 1978).
6. E. V. Clark, 'On the Acquisition of the Meaning of Before and After', *Journal of Verbal Learning and Verbal Behavior*, 1971, *10*, 266–75.
7. J. G. de Villiers, H. B. Tager-Flusberg, K. Hakuta and M. Cohen, 'Children's Comprehension of Relative Clauses', *Journal of Psycholinguistic Research*, forthcoming.
8. E. Pitcher and E. Prelinger, *Children Tell Stories* (New York: International Universities Press, 1963).
9. T. G. Bever, 'The Cognitive Basis for Linguistic Structures'. In J. R. Hayes, ed., *Cognition and the Development of Language* (New York: Wiley, 1970). J. G. de

Villiers and P. A. de Villiers, 'Development of the Use of Word Order in Comprehension', *Journal of Psycholinguistic Research*, 1973, *2*, 331–41.

10. M. P. Maratsos, 'How to Get from Words to Sentences'. In D. Aaronson and R. W. Rieber, eds., *Perspectives in Psycholinguistics* (Hillsdale, NJ: Lawrence Erlbaum Associates, 1978).

11. A. Sinclair, H. Sinclair and O. De Marcellus, 'Young Children's Comprehension and Production of Passive Sentences', *Archives de psychologie*, 1971, *61*, 1–20.

12. I. Brown, 'Role of Referent Concreteness in the Acquisition of Passive Sentence Comprehension Through Abstract Modeling', *Journal of Experimental Child Psychology*, 1976, *22*, 185–99.

6 FREEDOM OF SPEECH

1. R. F. Cromer, 'The Development of Language and Cognition: The Cognition Hypothesis'. In B. Foss, ed., *New Perspectives in Child Development* (Harmondsworth: Penguin Books, 1974).

2. D. I. Slobin, 'The Acquisition of Russian as a Native Language'. In F. Smith and G. A. Miller, eds., *The Genesis of Language: A Psycholinguistic Approach* (Cambridge: MIT Press, 1966).

3. J. Piaget, 'Piaget's Theory'. In P. H. Mussen, ed., *Carmichael's Manual of Child Psychology*, 3rd ed., vol. 1 (New York: Wiley, 1970).

4. J. H. Flavell, P. T. Botkin, C. C. Fry, J. W. Wright and P. E. Jarvis, *The Development of Role-Taking and Communication Skills in Children* (New York: Wiley, 1968).

5. M. P. Maratsos, *The Use of Definite and Indefinite Reference in Young Children: An Experimental Study of Semantic Acquisition* (Cambridge: Cambridge University Press, 1976).

6. D. J. Bruce, 'The Analysis of Word Sounds by Young Children', *British Journal of Educational Psychology*, 1964, *34*, 158–9.

7. R. H. Weir, *Language in the Crib* (The Hague: Mouton, 1962).

8. I. Papandrapoulou and H. Sinclair, 'What Is a Word? Experimental Study of Children's Ideas on Grammar', *Human Development*, 1974, *17*, 241–58. H. Wetstone, 'About Word Words and Thing Words: A Study of Metalinguistic Awareness'. Paper presented at Second Annual Boston University Conference on Language Development, 1977.

9. P. A. de Villiers and J. G. de Villiers, 'Early Judgments of Semantic and Syntactic Acceptability by Children', *Journal of Psycholinguistic Research*, 1972, *1*, 299–310.

10. F. Kessel, 'The Role of Syntax in Children's Comprehension from Ages 6–12', *Monographs of the Society for Research in Child Development*, 1970, *35*, No. 6.

11. B. Fowles and M. E. Glanz, 'Competence and Talent in Verbal Riddle Comprehension', *Journal of Child Language*, 1977, *4*, 433–52.

7 CRUCIAL EXPERIENCES

1. C. Ferguson and C. Snow, *Talking to Children: Language Input and Acquisition* (Cambridge: Cambridge University Press, 1977). J. G. de Villiers and P. A. de Villiers, 'Semantics and Syntax in the First Two Years: The Output of Form and Function and the Form and Function of the Input'. In F. D. Minifie and L. L. Lloyd, eds., *Communicative and Cognitive Abilities: Early Behavioral Assessment* (Baltimore: University Park Press, 1978).

2. J. D. Bohannon, A. Marquis, R. Storjohann and L. Boyer, 'A Child's Control of Motherese'. Paper presented at Society for Research in Child Development, New Orleans, 1977.

3. E. Newport, 'Motherese: The Speech of Mothers to Young Children'. In N. J. Castellan, D. B. Pisoni and G. Potts, eds., *Cognitive Theory*, vol. 2 (Hillsdale, NJ: Lawrence Erlbaum Associates, 1977).

4. R. W. Brown, C. Cazden and U. Bellugi, 'The Child's

Grammar from I to III'. In J. P. Hill, ed., *Minnesota Symposium on Child Psychology*, vol. 2 (Minneapolis: University of Minnesota Press, 1969).

5. C. E. Snow, A. Arlman-Rupp, Y. Hassing, J. Jobse, J. Joosken and J. Vorster, 'Mother's Speech in Three Social Classes', *Journal of Psycholinguistic Research*, 1976, *5*, 1–20.

6. B. Bard and J. Sachs, 'Language Acquisition Patterns in Two Normal Children of Deaf Parents'. Paper presented to the Second Annual Boston University Conference on Language Acquisition, October 1977.

7. C. B. Cazden, 'Environmental Assistance to the Child's Acquisition of Grammar' (diss., Harvard University, 1965). C. Feldman, 'The Effects of Various Types of Adult Responses in the Syntactic Acquisition of Two-to-Three-Year-Olds'. Unpublished paper, University of Chicago, 1971. J. L. Gonzales, 'The Effects of Maternal Stimulation on Early Language Development of Mexican-American Children', *Dissertation Abstracts*, 1973, *33* (7-A), 34–6.

8. K. E. Nelson, G. Carskaddon and J. D. Bonvillian, 'Syntax Acquisition: Impact of Experimental Variation in Adult Verbal Interaction with the Child', *Child Development*, 1973, *44*, 497–504. K. E. Nelson, 'Facilitating Syntax Acquisition'. Paper presented to the Eastern Psychological Association, New York, April 1975.

9. U. Bellugi, 'Learning the Language', *Psychology Today*, 1970, *4*, 32–5, 66.

10. R. W. Brown and C. Hanlon, 'Derivational Complexity and Order of Acquisition in Child Speech'. In J. R. Hayes, ed., *Cognition and the Development of Language* (New York: Wiley, 1970).

11. S. L. Harris, 'Teaching Language to Nonverbal Children: With Emphasis on Problems of Generalization', *Psychological Bulletin*, 1975, *82*, 565–80. D. Guess, W. Sailor and D. M. Baer, 'To Teach Language to Retarded Children'. In R. L. Schiefelbusch and L. L. Lloyd, eds., *Language Perspectives: Acquisition, Retardation and Intervention* (Baltimore: University Park Press, 1974).

8 CONSTRAINTS ON LEARNING

1. N. Chomsky, 'On the Nature of Language'. In S. R. Harnad, H. D. Steklis and J. Lancaster, eds., *Origins and Evolution of Language and Speech. Annals of the New York Academy of Sciences*, 1976, *280*, 46–55.

2. C. Hayes, *The Ape in Our House* (New York: Harper, 1951).

3. R. A. Gardner and B. T. Gardner, 'Teaching Sign Language to a Chimpanzee', *Science*, 1969, *165*, 664–72.

4. H. S. Terrace, L. Petitto and T. G. Bever, 'Project Nim: Progress Report II'. Unpublished paper, Columbia University, 1976.

5. D. Premack, *Intelligence in Ape and Man* (Hillsdale, NJ: Lawrence Erlbaum Associates, 1976). D. M. Rumbaugh, ed., *Language Learning by a Chimpanzee: The Lana Project* (New York and London: Academic Press, 1977).

6. E. H. Lenneberg, *Biological Foundations of Language* (New York: Wiley, 1967).

7. P. Marler, 'The Filtering of External Stimuli During Instinctive Behavior'. In W. H. Thorpe and O. L. Zangwill, eds., *Current Problems in Animal Behaviour* (Cambridge: Cambridge University Press, 1961).

8. E. H. Lenneberg, I. A. Nichols and E. R. Rosenberger, 'Primitive Stages of Language Development in Mongolism', *Disorders of Communication* (Research Publications, Association for Research in Nervous and Mental Disease), 1964, *42*, 119–37.

9. S. Krashen, 'The Critical Period for Language Acquisition and Its Possible Bases'. In D. Aaronson and R. W. Rieber, eds., *Developmental Psycholinguistics and Communication Disorders. Annals of the New York Academy of Sciences*, 1975, *263*, 211–24.

10. H. Lane, *The Wild Boy of Aveyron* (Cambridge: Harvard University Press, 1976).

11. S. Curtiss, *Genie: A Psycholinguistic Study of a Modern Day 'Wild Child'* (New York and London: Academic Press, 1977).

12. D. I. Slobin, 'Cognitive Prerequisites for the Development of Grammar'. In C. A. Ferguson and D. I. Slobin, eds., *Studies of Child Language Development* (New York: Holt, Rinehart and Winston, 1973).

13. R. W. Brown and C. Hanlon, 'Derivational Complexity and Order of Acquisition in Child Speech'. In J. R. Hayes, ed., *Cognition and the Development of Language* (New York: Wiley, 1970).

14. R. F. Cromer, 'The Development of Language and Cognition: The Cognition Hypothesis'. In B. Foss, ed., *New Perspectives in Child Development* (Harmondsworth: Penguin Books, 1974).

15. D. I. Slobin, 'The Acquisition of Russian as a Native Language'. In F. Smith and G. A. Miller, eds., *The Genesis of Language: A Psycholinguistic Approach* (Cambridge: MIT Press, 1966).

16. T. G. Bever, 'The Cognitive Basis for Linguistic Structures'. In J. R. Hayes, ed., *Cognition and the Development of Language* (New York: Wiley, 1970).

17. H. H. Clark and E. V. Clark, *Psychology and Language: An Introduction to Psycholinguistics* (New York: Harcourt Brace Jovanovich, 1977).

18. L. M. Bloom, L. Hood and P. Lightbown, 'Imitation in Language Development: If, When and Why', *Cognitive Psychology*, 1974, 6, 380–420.

19. K. Nelson, 'Structure and Strategy in Learning to Talk', *Monographs of the Society for Research in Child Development*, 1973, 38, No. 149.

Suggested Reading

Elizabeth Bates, *Language and Context: The Acquisition of Pragmatics* (New York and London: Academic Press, 1976). Provides a clear and comprehensive analysis of the uses of language in communication and traces the emergence of these functions in children's speech. Bates argues that pragmatics is central to any account of language development.

Roger Brown, *A First Language: The Early Stages* (Cambridge: Harvard University Press, 1973; London: Allen & Unwin, 1973). This classic book brings together data on children learning several different languages to argue for certain universal characteristics of the relational meanings expressed in the first sentences. Brown studied three children over the course of their language development and provides a detailed account of their early grammatical rule learning.

Jill G. de Villiers and Peter A. de Villiers, *Language Acquisition* (Cambridge: Harvard University Press, 1978). A comprehensive introduction to the field of language acquisition, this volume is a little more technical than the present book and provides more discussion of theoretical and linguistic issues in the field. The book deals centrally with the way the child acquires the sounds, meanings, and grammar of his language, and the way he learns to use language to communicate with others. It includes a thorough survey of the disorders of language characteristic of deaf, retarded, dysphasic, and autistic children.

Charles A. Ferguson and Daniel I. Slobin, eds., *Studies of Child Language Development* (New York: Holt, Rinehart and Winston, 1973). A carefully edited volume of papers covering the acquisition of the sounds and grammar of language. The book is particularly valuable since it gathers together work on the acquisition of many different languages and contains papers that are not readily available from other sources. The comments by the editors that introduce each section are helpful and serve to highlight the important issues.

Charles A. Ferguson and Catherine E. Snow, eds., *Talking to Children: Language Input and Acquisition* (Cambridge: Cambridge University Press, 1977). An excellent collection of the latest research on mothers' speech to children and its possible effects on the child's language. The book covers a wide range of different languages and societies and adds much to our understanding of the context in which the child learns language.

Donald M. Morehead and Ann E. Morehead, eds., *Normal and Deficient Language* (Baltimore: University Park Press, 1976). This book contains several outstanding reviews of the normal child's acquisition of sounds, meanings, and the use of lauguage, plus an account of the relationship between intellectual and language development. Other chapters describe the language of deaf, dysphasic, and retarded children.

Richard L. Schiefelbusch and Lyle L. Lloyd, eds., *Language Perspectives: Acquisition, Retardation and Intervention* (Baltimore: University Park Press, 1974). An important collection of essays by leading authors in the field summarizing what is known about the acquisition of speech sounds, grammar, and word meaning in normal and retarded children. The book is particularly valuable for the chapters describing programmes to train language to deaf, retarded, and autistic children.

Index

Index

Fontana Paperbacks: Non-fiction

Fontana is a leading paperback publisher of non-fiction, both popular and academic. Below are some recent titles.

- [ ] AN AUTOBIOGRAPHY Peter Alliss £1·95
- [ ] BOB HOPE: PORTRAIT OF A SUPERSTAR Charles Thompson £1·75

- [ ] SUBJECT WOMEN Ann Oakley £2·75
- [ ] HOW TO GET RID OF THE BOMB Gavin Scott £1·95
- [ ] POLICEMAN'S PATCH Harry Cole £1·50
- [ ] A YEAR IN THE DRINK Martin Green £1·75
- [ ] SCOTLAND introduction by Lord Home £4·95
- [ ] THE NO-DIET BOOK Michael Spira £1·50
- [ ] SIR JAMES GOLDSMITH Geoffrey Wansell £1·95
- [ ] THE CINDERELLA COMPLEX Colette Dowling £1·75
- [ ] DIANA, THE PRINCESS OF WALES Hugh Montgomery-Massingberd £1·95
- [ ] SONIA ALLISON'S FOOD PROCESSOR COOKBOOK £1·95
- [ ] THE ENTERTAINING COOKBOOK Evelyn Rose £3·95
- [ ] WAR AND SOCIETY IN REVOLUTIONARY EUROPE 1770–1870 Geoffrey Best £2·95
- [ ] EUROPEAN EMPIRES FROM CONQUEST TO COLLAPSE 1815–1960 Victor Kiernan £2·95
- [ ] DARWIN Wilma George £1·75
- [ ] THIS IS WINDSURFING Reinhart Winkler £5·95
- [ ] CHAMPION'S STORY Bob Champion & Jonathan Powell £1·50

You can buy Fontana paperbacks at your local bookshop or newsagent. Or you can order them from Fontana Paperbacks, Cash Sales Department, Box 29, Douglas, Isle of Man. Please send a cheque, postal or money order (not currency) worth the purchase price plus 10p per book (or plus 12p per book if outside the UK).

NAME (Block letters) _____

ADDRESS _____

_____

_____